HUSTLE
FROM THE
HEART

A PATH *to* **SUCCESS** *for*
FEELERS, HEALERS, *and*
SENSITIVE ENTREPRENEURS

JOSHUA ROSENTHAL, MScED

WONDERWELL
PRESS

Published by Wonderwell Press
Austin, Texas
www.gbgpress.com

This work is being published under the Wonderwell Press imprint by an
exclusive arrangement with Wonderwell. Wonderwell, Wonderwell Press,
and the Wonderwell logos are wholly-owned trademarks of Wonderwell.

Distributed by Greenleaf Book Group

For ordering information or special discounts for bulk purchases, please
contact Greenleaf Book Group at PO Box 91869, Austin, TX 78709,
512.891.6100.

Design and composition by Greenleaf Book Group
Cover design by Greenleaf Book Group
Cover images used under license from ©Adobestock.com

Publisher's Cataloging-in-Publication data is available.

Print ISBN: 978-1-963827-32-3

eBook ISBN: 978-1-963827-36-1

First Edition

CONTENTS

FOREWORD

Sixteen years ago, I had a vision: to create a lifestyle brand rooted in wellness, transparency, and real nourishment. What I didn't have? A background in food manufacturing, a business plan, or any clue how to get a product onto a grocery store shelf. What I did have was a gut feeling—and, perhaps more importantly, the early guidance and inspiration I received from Joshua Rosenthal.

When I completed my health coach training at the Institute for Integrative Nutrition, Joshua's teachings stayed with me in a way I didn't fully understand at the time. I thought I would be a nutrition counselor, working one-on-one with clients. And for a while, I did just that. But a turning point came when I baked a batch of blueberry muffins for a local race in New York, hoping to attract interest in my counseling services. No one wanted to sign up for nutrition coaching—but everyone wanted the muffins.

That moment, as small as it was, shifted everything. I could have ignored it or brushed it off as a fluke. But something Joshua often said echoed in my mind: "Feel the fear, and do it anyway." That became a personal mantra. I leaned into the unknown, into scrappiness, and into instinct.

From my Upper West Side apartment, I began selling baking

mixes. I hand-delivered them to natural food stores and shipped orders myself. My first granola recipe—still unchanged today—was born in that same tiny kitchen. I invested $5,000 of personal savings into the first production run, not knowing what would come of it. By 2013, we were being pushed into national distribution by Whole Foods. I remember crying on the subway after reading the email. It was the kind of moment that catches you off guard but also confirms that you're on the right path.

Today, Purely Elizabeth is in more than thirty thousand stores across the country, with more than $200 million in annual revenue. We've received major investments and built out a dream team, yet—at our core—we're still guided by the same principles that fueled those early days: lead with purpose, trust your intuition, and create something that serves people's lives.

So much of that mindset was seeded by Joshua.

When he asked me to write the foreword for this book, I was honored—but also deeply moved. Joshua has played such a quiet but powerful role in my journey, and I know I'm not alone in that. What he offers in *Hustle from the Heart* is something rare in the world of business books: permission to lead with empathy—to build not by becoming someone else but by becoming *more* of who you already are.

In these pages, Joshua shows you that being sensitive, thoughtful, or heart led isn't a liability; it's your edge. His voice is steady and generous. He's been in the trenches, and he shares his wisdom not from a pedestal but from beside you. He understands the chaos and beauty of starting something from scratch—of building something deeply personal while staying grounded in service.

Reading this book, I saw so many of the lessons I lived through reflected back to me: stepping outside your comfort zone, trusting imperfect action, allowing the vision to evolve, and surrounding yourself with people who see your potential before you fully do. It reminded me of the years I worked without outside investment because I wanted to hold onto the soul of the company. The times I led with intuition rather than strategy. The moments I had to quiet the noise and go back to my "why."

Hustle from the Heart is for anyone who feels called to do things differently. It's a guidebook for the dreamers, healers, and feelers who don't see themselves in the usual entrepreneurship success stories—and don't want to become hardened in order to succeed.

Joshua's story and his way of teaching affirm that your softness, your sensitivity, your deep desire to help others—these are your superpowers. His journey with the Institute for Integrative Nutrition was proof of that for me when I was just getting started. And now, this book can be that proof for you.

Read it with a pen in hand and an open heart. Let it challenge you. Let it soothe you. Let it remind you that the bravest kind of success is the kind that stays true to your soul. Then get out there and build something beautiful.

—ELIZABETH STEIN
Founder and CEO, Purely Elizabeth

INTRODUCTION

Do you feel a deep calling to make a difference in the world but struggle to turn that passion into a thriving business? You're not alone. As the founder of the Institute for Integrative Nutrition (IIN), I've seen countless coaches, healers, and creatives face this exact problem.

These individuals—maybe you're one of them—are some of the most caring, sensitive, and passionate people on the planet. They're empathetic, purpose-driven, and dedicated to helping others. Yet when it comes to the business side of things, they freeze up. Marketing their services? Awkward. Having money talks with potential clients? Terrifying.

Fear and self-doubt hold them back from even starting. Others launch their businesses but get stuck, unsure of how to take the next step. The result? They undervalue themselves, miss out on financial abundance, and procrastinate going after their dreams.

If you're nodding along, I'm here to tell you it doesn't have to be this way.

As a highly sensitive person myself, I understand how intimidating entrepreneurship can feel. So many people out there want to "crush the competition," and you and I are wired differently. But here's the thing: You don't need to become a shark to succeed. You can build a thriving business without selling your soul. That's the heart of this book: learning to "hustle from the heart." It's about building a thriving business without losing your sensitivity. Trust me; I've done it.

Thirty years ago, I was a broke forty-year-old with no idea what I was doing, just holding onto a wild idea about starting a nutrition school. The field of health coaching didn't even exist yet, but I saw a major gap in the healthcare industry: People needed guidance on nutrition and emotional well-being that traditional doctors simply weren't providing. So I rented an office in New York City. For the first few years, I couldn't afford rent, so I slept on a couch in the office of the school. I didn't have an MBA or a business plan, but I believed in my vision. I followed my heart and intuition, and I learned how to balance that with grit, hard work, and determination. Now, IIN is the largest nutrition school in the world, health coaching has grown into a billion-dollar industry, and I get to give back in ways I never imagined.

How did I do it? I'll be sharing all the unconventional secrets that helped me get to where I am today—including things I've never shared publicly before. You'll learn how to

- Question traditional ideas of success to define what truly matters to you
- Find challenges that energize rather than drain you
- Build mental strength to overcome obstacles and setbacks
- Create a business that fits your unique personality and values
- Leverage your natural strengths to stand out in the marketplace
- Let go of perfectionism that keeps you stuck

- Trust your intuition and recognize synchronicity in business opportunities
- Develop an authentic brand that attracts your ideal audience
- Value your services and price them with confidence
- Connect with clients who appreciate what you offer
- Stay calm and focused when facing business challenges
- Keep growing your business through continuous learning

This isn't your typical business book. No boring theories or corporate jargon here. Just practical advice and mindset shifts that work for real people.

It's for the feelers, healers, creatives, and sensitive souls who are tired of the nine-to-five grind and want to thrive. It's for the dreamers and the doers with big visions. It's for those who are committed to making their mark on the world, even if they're not quite sure how to do it yet. Whether you're ready to dive headfirst into full-time entrepreneurship or you're looking to grow a serious side hustle, you'll find something useful here.

I'm not going to teach you how to get rich quick or work two hours a week from the beach. But as someone who's mentored countless empaths and sensitive strivers over the years, I know the last thing you need is another path to burnout. You're already juggling so much—maybe raising a family, caring for aging parents, or supporting everyone else's dreams while putting your own on hold. On top of that, many aspiring health coaches and new entrepreneurs get caught up in perfecting their website or crafting the ideal Instagram post, thinking that's what building a business looks like.

They hesitate to do the real work of finding clients because it feels uncomfortable or they're not sure where to start.

I understand: When your nature is to nurture, the boundary setting and self-promotion that business requires can feel foreign or even wrong. But there's a better way forward, one that doesn't require you to sacrifice your well-being or become someone you're not. Building something meaningful does take effort, but it shouldn't drain the very energy and compassion that make you exceptional at what you do. This journey is about self-discovery and growth, finding the courage to be true to yourself while developing the practical skills to turn your calling into a thriving business.

If you're ready to embrace your sensitivity as a strength, to challenge the conventional wisdom about what it takes to succeed, and to build a business that's authentically you, you're in the right place. I see you, I understand your struggles, and I believe in your potential. Together, we'll explore how you can not only prosper but thrive, on your own terms, by leading with your beautiful, compassionate heart.

1
—

QUESTION WHAT YOU'VE BEEN TAUGHT

I was an average student in school. While others seemed to thrive in structure, I felt bored and out of place. Algebra in ninth grade seemed pointless; I didn't get why it mattered in the scheme of things, and I just couldn't grasp it. I skipped the final exam because I knew I'd probably fail anyway. At some point, I accepted that my brain was wired differently. School was not unlocking my full potential.

Outside of school, I didn't quite fit the mold either. Raised in a close-knit Orthodox Jewish community in Toronto, Canada, I watched my parents, both Holocaust survivors, work tirelessly to build a good life for our family. While I deeply appreciated their devotion, I often felt confined by the strict rules and rituals of our faith.

In our insular community, the focus was always on the

uniqueness of our Jewish heritage, not only stretching back thousands of years but also carrying profound biblical and ancient significance. However, as I grew older, I began to question this narrative. I sensed there was a deeper truth beyond what I had been taught, and I developed a strong desire to broaden my horizons, explore different perspectives, and connect with the wider world beyond my community.

As a teenager, this search for understanding led me to devour hundreds of nonfiction books. From Eastern philosophy to Western science, I consumed it all. Hungry for knowledge and fresh points of view, I searched for answers to questions I didn't yet know how to ask.

Eventually, I met someone—a rabbi—who truly understood how to help me. He got me into graduate school by using my extensive religious studies as undergraduate work, and before I knew it, I had a master's degree by the time I was twenty. People who know me call this "classic Joshua"—always finding creative ways to work the system!

But this was just the start of my journey. After graduate school, I took a leap into the unknown and joined a spiritual community in Berkeley, California, called the Aquarian Minyan. To say it was a culture shock would be an understatement. This environment was the polar opposite of the sheltered, insular world I grew up in— open, carefree, and a little wild. I had no idea how to operate in an anything-goes type of setting, but I welcomed the discomfort, knowing it would push me to grow.

Eager to expand my consciousness, I explored different holistic practices in California. One in particular—Rolfing—completely altered the way I viewed the world. Rolfing is a form of bodywork that realigns the body's structure through deep manipulation of the fascia, the connective tissue around muscles and organs. Practitioners use their hands to apply pressure and movement, working to release tension patterns and improve the body's alignment, flexibility, and overall function.

During one session, the practitioner focused on my pineal gland, sometimes called the third eye or God spot. He used a finger cot to do very deep work on the palette of my mouth, then up my nose, connecting with my brain's nervous system.

Immediately afterward, time lost its meaning. I walked outside and just stood there, like I had nowhere to go and nothing to do for the rest of my life. I felt grounded in the present moment and connected to something greater than myself.

This crack in the cosmic egg experience changed something in me. I guess I must have seemed different, because my parents back in Canada started to worry. During one long-distance phone call, my mother suggested I come home to rest. But after boarding the plane back to Toronto, I panicked. If I went home, I'd be stuck again in a life that felt limiting. In that moment, something crystallized: I could no longer conform to the expectations others had imposed on me. I got off the plane before it took off.

A week later, my mother flew to California to check on me, and I panicked again. Her presence felt suffocating, reminding me of my restrictive childhood. Desperate to avoid her, I left the campus with just the clothes on my back—no money, no ID. I just needed to wander alone, to search for truth on my own terms.

What followed nearly killed me.

I ended up on some guy's private property, and he called the police. When the officers arrived and learned that I had no form of identification, they told me I was under arrest.

"What did I do?" I asked, genuinely curious.

"You're trespassing on private property, and we have no way of knowing who you are," one officer replied.

"I'm just me," I said, then added, "How do I know who *you* are?"

They took me to the police station and put me in jail. My confusion and fear led me to cause a disruption, which only made things worse. Soon, I found myself strapped to a stretcher, loaded into a police van, and taken to a psychiatric hospital. There, they injected me with drugs against my will.

The next thing I remember is waking up restrained in an all-white room. I thought I had died and gone to heaven, because I couldn't move or feel anything. The medication had put me in an altered state; I was basically a vegetable.

Thankfully, my dear mother searched for me, going from one police station to another and filing missing persons reports until she finally found me and got me released on the condition that I go to a private psychiatric facility. Once there, they diagnosed me with schizophrenia. Doctors said I was incurably ill and my mental illness would forever limit me. All the while, I didn't believe them. Deep inside, I knew there was nothing wrong with me.

Eventually, I saw a psychiatrist named Dr. Klein. He was the first person who actually talked to me and asked me what happened. As I shared my story, he listened. Then, he said what I needed to hear: "There's nothing wrong with you. You don't have schizophrenia. You're having a spiritual experience. You aren't a danger to yourself or society. You're free to go."

Once I could be on my own again, I traveled the world, continuing my spiritual quest. I visited temples and ashrams across Asia, immersing myself in different cultures and spiritual traditions. I learned along the way that normal is subjective depending on where you go. What's considered normal in one culture can be vastly different in another.

So, what is truly true? With so many different religions and ways of life, which one is right? I wrestled with these questions, realizing that most of what I'd been taught was biased or incomplete. I mean, we're all just floating on a rock in space. None of us knows what happens after we die. So why do so many people pretend to have all the answers?

Though my unconventional path exposed me to some darkness, it also led me to my inner light. It taught me to question external authority and trust my instincts. The more I followed my gut, the less I struggled, and my life improved.

Before founding IIN, I studied nutrition and did health counseling. Studying nutrition, I was confronted again with a maze of conflicting theories. Everyone had a different opinion about what we should and shouldn't be eating. And they were all religiously certain that their way was the right way. Again, I had to cut through the noise and find my own truth. I experimented with different diets to see how each made me feel. I paid attention to my energy, cravings, moods, and symptoms. Over time, I found what worked for me. This taught me that there's no one-size-fits-all approach to eating—or to anything. We are each the experts of our own experience.

When I started IIN in the early 1990s, I was thirty-eight and broke. I had no business plan. But I had a calling—a vision to create a holistic nutrition school that would empower people to listen to their bodies, honor their individual truths, and take charge of their health.

This idea came to me in part because I noticed a major gap in the healthcare system. Busy doctors treated symptoms and prescribed medication rather than seeing the whole picture of patients' lives. What people needed was for someone to listen to them, show compassion, and help them get to the root cause of their issues.

So with no capital, I followed my heart. I rented a tiny office in New York City and started teaching classes. My curriculum combined multiple dietary theories because no single approach works for everyone. I encouraged students to experiment and listen to their bodies. I taught them that everything is food—not just what we eat, but what we feed our hearts and minds. It's all connected.

Many were skeptical and doubted the school would last, but my purpose kept me going. I believed people needed this knowledge. I was right. The classes grew quickly. IIN became a pioneering force, part of a movement that redefined health and nutrition.

Decades later, IIN has become the world's largest nutrition school. With more than 150,000 graduates in 175 countries, IIN continues to empower students to find food freedom and transform their lives.

SUCCESS ON YOUR TERMS

You might be wondering, *What does all this have to do with me and my business?* Everything. By following my calling and staying true to myself, I built an impactful organization that defied expectations. IIN grew into something bigger than anyone imagined possible. And if I can do it, you can too—by trusting yourself and not conforming to others' limited beliefs.

The journey to authentic success often means choosing to fit *out* rather than fit in—spiritually, financially, and in how you live your life. In India, I learned from teachers who emphasized creating your own path, even if it meant breaking from tradition. They taught that while family is precious, we shouldn't let others' expectations stop us from following our deeper calling.

The real challenge comes when we question conventional definitions of success: money, status, and external validation. These are often the markers society tells us to strive for. But what if your definition is different? What if success, for you, means inner peace, creative freedom, or the ability to make a meaningful impact? How will you know you've reached it? You'll know because your life will feel aligned with your deepest values and passions.

This isn't always easy. Family and cultural expectations, though often well-meaning, can hold us back. There's often pressure to follow a set path: Get a stable job, marry at the right age, have kids, buy a house. This is all fine if it's what you want. But what if your soul is calling you somewhere else? What if your version of success looks different?

True success isn't about checking boxes; it's about living a life that feels authentically fulfilling to you.

THE ART OF UNLEARNING

We each have a unique purpose. When we're brave enough to honor it, we can transform our lives and the world around us. First, though, we must unlearn the limiting beliefs we've picked up along the way. This unlearning is key to finding our true calling.

Unlearning means bringing awareness to beliefs we've internalized that no longer serve us. It means questioning what we're told, thinking for ourselves, and trusting our intuition instead of accepting everything at face value.

In my twenties, seeking spiritual wisdom meant surrendering to the unknown and letting go of what I thought I knew. This deprogramming helped me discover an authentic path forward. We all go through life accumulating knowledge and beliefs that shape our worldview. Some help us navigate life, but some end up limiting us. That's why we need to examine our biases, assumptions, and what we take for granted as truth.

For example, maybe you learned in school that grades measure intelligence. But is this a fact? Many successful entrepreneurs, including me, didn't do well in school. Good grades don't measure intelligence any more than they measure discipline and conscientiousness. So this foundational "truth" might be flawed. In the process of examining individual beliefs, ask yourself, *What evidence supports this belief? What evidence contradicts it?* This helps clear out restrictive thought patterns and replace them with beliefs that help you grow.

Unlearning also involves examining the wisdom we receive from our families and communities. Although there's value in traditional knowledge, we need to question whether these inherited beliefs truly serve us. Sometimes, the most loving thing we can do—for ourselves and our families—is break free from limiting patterns, even when it's uncomfortable. This act of breaking free is loving because it allows us to honor our authentic selves and can inspire positive change in those around us. By courageously pursuing our own path, we often expand what's possible—not just for ourselves but for future generations of our family.

A huge part of unlearning is critical thinking, which requires taking in information objectively and evaluating sources before accepting ideas as facts. With so many self-proclaimed experts today, we really need to probe deeper, do our own research, and consider different views. Even credentialed authorities can have blind spots, biases, or hidden motives that influence their perspectives.

Unlearning is not about throwing out everything you've ever learned; it's about critically examining your beliefs and keeping only what truly serves you, so you can create a life that aligns with your purpose and values.

DEBUNKING COMMON SUCCESS MYTHS

Now that we've explored the importance of unlearning, let's tackle some common misconceptions about success. Society feeds us many stories about what it takes to make it—stories that often hold us back or lead us down paths that don't align with our true selves. By examining and debunking these myths, we can free ourselves to pursue success on our own terms.

MYTH 1: YOU NEED A FORMAL EDUCATION TO BE SUCCESSFUL

Many people think you need an advanced degree to be successful. While degrees help in certain fields, they don't guarantee you'll learn the practical skills needed to make it in the real world. Often, raw experience teaches you more.

Look at people like Mark Zuckerberg, Bill Gates, and Sara Blakely—they all dropped out of school and built massive companies. My friend Michael Ellsberg wrote a book called *The Education of Millionaires*, in which he interviewed self-made business geniuses without college degrees. Most of them said the same thing: School doesn't teach the critical skills for success.

I saw this at IIN when we had many employees with advanced degrees. Surprisingly, this was one of our least successful periods. These employees focused on theoretical concepts from their MBA programs instead of addressing the practical needs of the business. They thought their education made them smarter than me, so they often ignored my guidance. Many of them viewed IIN as just a stepping stone in their careers, focusing more on padding their resumes than on driving real results for the company.

On paper, they looked impressive. But they lacked the creativity and drive that comes from real experience. That's why I prefer working with people who are street smart—those who take initiative and think on their feet. They're the ones who move the needle and get things done.

Recently, a family friend's son told me he wanted to go to school to study real estate development. "No!" I said. "Get a job with a real estate developer instead. Here's why: A, you won't have to pay for it; B, you'll get paid while you learn; and C, you'll learn the real, tactical stuff that matters in the field."

Before investing in education, think about faster, cheaper ways to gain practical skills. Want to open a spa? Don't take a course; go work for someone who owns one. Notice what mistakes they're making, and try to avoid them. Then, when you're ready, take what you've learned and start your own.

This works for almost any field. Shadow an expert, or start in an entry-level role in the field you want to break into. Be resourceful, learn by doing, and find mentors who can share insider knowledge on what really leads to success in a given industry.

MYTH 2: IT'S ALL LUCK

Many believe that success is just being in the right place at the right time. But success rarely comes from luck alone. Sure, I've had lucky breaks I call serendipity, but those moments were also the result of hard work, persistence, and personal sacrifice.

Think about those overnight success stories you hear in the media. Dig a little deeper, and you'll usually find people who spent years honing their craft and putting in the effort to reach that point. Their success might seem sudden, but it's usually the result of a long journey with many ups and downs.

I've lived this. When IIN was on the brink of getting shut down, luck didn't save us. I pushed myself to superhuman limits to keep it afloat. This meant sacrificing my health and working relentlessly, but those hours got us over the line. It wasn't luck; it was grit and determination.

My parents taught me this too. As Holocaust survivors who immigrated to Canada with nothing, not even speaking English, they faced incredible hardships but kept pushing forward to build a life for our family. Day after day, I watched them come home from work exhausted. I get emotional even thinking about it now. Their experience showed me that success requires great sacrifice.

Let me be clear: I'm not advocating that you work yourself to exhaustion. The goal is to choose challenges that excite and motivate you. Balance hard work with self-care. But understand that reaching your goals will require some sacrifice. You've got to be prepared to keep pushing forward even when things get tough, build your skills day by day, and take action consistently. While it's great when luck comes your way, don't wait for it.

MYTH 3: GRINDING HARD GUARANTEES SUCCESS

Hard work definitely matters, but grinding without purpose or strategy is like trying to chop down a tree with a butter knife: You'll wear yourself out before you see real progress. Success isn't just about putting in hours; it's about working smart, focusing on what truly moves the needle, and maintaining balance.

In a world where achievement is glorified, many people chase material success and accolades believing it will bring fulfillment—only to find that it often comes at the cost of inner peace. I've met plenty of hustle-culture entrepreneurs who sacrificed everything to build their businesses, only to end up disconnected from their families, facing health issues, and sitting alone in their fancy houses. Is that really success?

On the flip side, I've also seen many health coaches pour so much energy into perfecting their self-care routines that their businesses fall to the wayside. The advice I give to this group is that health is a vehicle, not a destination. If you're already healthier than 90 percent of Americans but your bank account is lacking, maybe it's time to shift some of that wellness energy into building your business.

Both of these approaches miss the mark. If you're burning the candle at both ends, you might reach your destination, but you'll be too exhausted to enjoy it. And if you've mastered making the perfect green juice but can't pay your bills, that's not where you want to be either.

The goal is harmony across all areas of life: health, finances, relationships, etc. Focusing entirely on one area while neglecting the others leads to imbalance. Remember the children's book *Hope for the Flowers*? Two caterpillars climb a tall pillar in pursuit of something more. One sacrifices everything to reach the top. The other listens to her intuition, stops climbing, and transforms into a butterfly. The lesson? Neither grinding endlessly nor waiting passively gets you where you need to go. Sometimes, success is about transformation and growth.

Many people spend their lives chasing an ever-moving finish line, following arbitrary benchmarks that don't actually reflect what they want. They get caught up chasing an idealized version of success without questioning why they're running so hard or what they're really after. As a result, they experience constant stress and anxiety about not being "there" yet—wherever "there" is supposed to be.

So what's the answer? Find your calling, push yourself beyond your comfort zone, and blend mindful intention with dedicated effort. Stay passionate about where you're going, understand why getting there matters to you personally, and be ready to put in the work—while keeping enough balance in your life to make the whole journey worthwhile.

MYTH 4: YOU MUST ADOPT A
DIFFERENT PERSONA TO SUCCEED

As someone quiet and introspective, I used to think that outgoing, opinionated people were smarter than me. Their confidence made me assume they knew what they were talking about. But often, this isn't the case. Many people project confidence without competence—sometimes to sell something or to maintain a certain image.

If you're a sensitive introvert like me, you might feel pressured to be more extroverted or salesy in business. But qualities like empathy and emotional intelligence are even more valuable. They enable us to understand and connect with clients and customers on a deep, authentic level. Different environments might seem to favor certain personalities, but we all have unique gifts to offer.

If being introverted or highly sensitive makes you question your potential, remember: These differences can be powerful assets when used strategically. The very qualities that make you question yourself can make you the go-to expert in your field.

MYTH 5: YOU MUST KNOW
EVERYTHING ABOUT EVERYTHING

Impostor syndrome is a common struggle for new entrepreneurs, especially health coaches. Many feel they don't know enough to be taken seriously or don't look the part. This self-doubt often prevents talented people from even starting.

But think about how the field of health coaching has evolved. Thirty years ago, when the field was just emerging, coaches doubted themselves even more. They wondered how an online course could prepare them to help people improve their health when doctors train for over a decade. Despite those doubts, the field has grown enormously, proving that health coaches can trust their abilities—even when mainstream medicine doesn't fully validate them. Healers and empaths often know more than they give themselves credit for. And the space they hold for others through active, empathetic listening is invaluable on its own.

The reality is, no expert—in any field—knows everything. You won't have all the answers up front, and that's okay. Being a pioneer means leveraging your current knowledge and strengths while being willing to learn and grow along the way. The most important step is to begin.

MYTH 6: YOU HAVE TO BE RUTHLESS

Some think success means being cutthroat and stepping on others to get ahead. This myth suggests that nice guys finish last and compassion has no place in the business world. However, my experience has shown me this isn't true.

Throughout my career, building relationships, mentoring others, and fostering community have been crucial for long-term success. At IIN, some of our biggest breakthroughs came from collaboration and mutual support, not ruthless competition.

This doesn't mean never being assertive or standing up for yourself. There are times when you need to put your interests first. But the most sustainable and fulfilling success comes from balancing drive with compassion and collaboration.

Many new entrepreneurs struggle with this, thinking they need to be aggressive in their marketing or client interactions. They worry that being too nice will make them seem unprofessional or ineffective. But the entrepreneurs who really thrive are those who lean into their natural empathy and use it as a strength. They build deep, trusting relationships with their clients, leading to better outcomes and more referrals. They also build connections with peer support or other business owners in their community, which strengthens their networks and provides ongoing opportunities.

Instead of being ruthless, be authentically you. Use your strengths, including your capacity for kindness and collaboration. Look for ways to lift others up as you climb. In the long run, this approach feels better and creates a more lasting impact.

MYTH 7: LATE BLOOMERS WON'T BLOOM

Society loves early success stories. We all hear about young entrepreneurs who hit it big in their twenties. But late bloomers aren't as rare as you may think.

Vera Wang entered the fashion industry at forty. Julia Child published her first cookbook at fifty. Ray Kroc opened the first McDonald's at fifty-two. Lucille Ball was forty when the first episode of *I Love Lucy* aired. Martha Stewart launched her media empire in her forties, turning her passion for home living into a billion-dollar brand. I began IIN at thirty-eight. And others bloomed even later—Colonel Sanders franchised KFC at sixty-two. Laura Ingalls Wilder published her first *Little House* book at sixty-five. Morgan Freeman got his big break at fifty-two, with fame growing well into his sixties and beyond.

We all have our own timeline. Not making it young doesn't mean the window has closed. Consistent effort over time matters most. Late bloomers often have more resilience and wisdom gained from experience. It's never too late to bloom. The only real deadline is the one you set for yourself.

MYTH 8: IT'S ALL ABOUT WEALTH AND STATUS

Our culture pushes the idea that success is measured by the size of your bank account or the prestige of your job title. Social media, magazines, and other media constantly reinforce this.

Having experienced both wealth and having very little, I can tell you that money doesn't buy happiness. Don't get me wrong: Financial stability matters, and wealth can make life easier. It provides security and opens up opportunities, but it's a means to an end, not an end itself. I've met millionaires who were anxious and unhappy because they had no real sense of meaning. And I've known people with modest incomes who were deeply fulfilled because they loved their work and spent time with people they cared about.

These success myths can be comforting because they offer clear rules to follow: Get the right degree, work the longest hours, and act a certain way. But real success rarely fits into such neat boxes. Once we let go of these limiting stories, we create space to write our own definitions of success—ones that actually reflect who we are and what matters most to us.

REFLECTION QUESTIONS

1. What beliefs about success did you inherit that may no longer serve you?

2. When have you trusted your intuition against conventional wisdom?

3. Which success myth has most influenced your choices?

4. What unique qualities do you possess that traditional definitions of success might undervalue?

5. How would you define success if no one else's opinion mattered?

2

—

FIND THE RIGHT
KIND OF HARD

Not all challenges are created equal. Some drain us, while others energize us. Some lead to dead ends, while others spark growth. The key isn't avoiding difficulty; it's choosing the right kind of hard. The challenges you take on should stretch you toward your potential while keeping you aligned with your values.

Just as athletes carefully select training regimens that help them grow stronger, entrepreneurs must be intentional about the challenges they take on. The right challenges build you up and move you closer to your vision while the wrong ones lead to burnout. When you pursue something that genuinely matters to you, obstacles become opportunities for growth instead of roadblocks.

Think about marathon runners. Running 26.2 miles is demanding, yet they persist because they've chosen this challenge intentionally. They've decided that crossing that finish line matters to them. The same applies to entrepreneurship. If you're pursuing a business idea that doesn't genuinely excite you or align with your values, you'll likely give up when things get tough. But when you're building something meaningful—something that connects to your heart's calling—you'll find strength you didn't know you had. This sense of purpose keeps you going through the ups and downs, helps you overcome challenges, and empowers you to build something that lasts.

Building a heart-centered business starts with reconnecting to the parts of yourself you've set aside—dreams you tucked away when life got busy, passions you labeled as impractical, or gifts you didn't recognize as valuable. Discovering your authentic purpose often requires tuning out the noise of daily tasks and others' expectations long enough to hear your own inner voice. But it's not just about rediscovering these dreams; it's about aligning them with real-world needs. When you match your natural gifts and deepest passions with problems that need solving, you create opportunities that are both meaningful and financially sustainable.

And that's the essence of the right kind of hard—the kind that brings growth, prosperity, and impact, along with the deeper reward of alignment that resonates with your soul.

DISCOVERING YOUR NATURAL GIFTS

Let's start with a simple but powerful question: What were you born to do? Not what others told you to do—whether that's what your parents, teachers, or your partner thinks would be practical—but what would bring you so much joy that it could add ten years to your life just because you love doing it?

Think of your natural gifts as your personal superpower—something that comes so naturally to you that you might not even recognize it as special. Maybe you have an uncanny ability to explain complex ideas simply, or perhaps you instinctively know how to make people feel heard and understood. These superpowers often hide in plain sight because they're such an integral part of who you are. They're the things you do effortlessly while others struggle—the talents that make people say, "How did you do that?" when, to you, it feels as natural as breathing.

Think back to your childhood and teenage years. What activities made you lose track of time? What dreams did you hold on to before the world told you to be realistic? What topics could you talk about for hours without getting bored? These early passions often hold the key to our natural talents.

If you're having trouble seeing your own unique gifts clearly, it can be helpful to ask for perspective from the people who know you well. Just as some people experience body dysmorphia and struggle to see their true image in the mirror, we can develop a distorted view of our own abilities and potential. Our view can be clouded by ego, past hurts, defense mechanisms, and even the way our brains are wired. No matter how intelligent we are, others often see things about us that we can't see ourselves.

That's why feedback from others is so important. It's often the missing piece in understanding our true strengths. Try this simple exercise to gather insights:

EXERCISE: THE HONEST ASSESSMENT

Ask five people who know you well to rate you on a scale of 1-10 in the following areas. Choose individuals you genuinely trust—those with good character, relevant experience, and judgment you respect. Ideally, include people from different spheres of your life (professional colleagues, longtime friends, and family members) to get diverse perspectives.

- Work drive and determination
- Creativity and innovation
- Sensitivity to others' needs
- Leadership abilities
- Problem-solving skills
- Communication style

Then, ask them these specific questions:

- What would you say is my greatest strength?
- What problems or challenges have you seen me solve effectively for you or others?
- What entrepreneurial qualities do you see in me?
- What field or industry do you think I'm best suited for?
- What's one blind spot you think I might have?

The answers may surprise you and help reveal patterns you've missed. But remember: Getting feedback is only part of the equation; how you process and apply it is another. When someone gives you feedback, how do you respond? Many of us hear feedback as criticism and instinctively resist it. The trick is to set your ego aside and listen with curiosity.

Input from others becomes especially valuable when evaluating business ideas. It's easy to get caught up in the adrenaline and self-love of pursuing your passion, but sometimes, it's a trap. Passion is powerful, but if you're not careful, it can create problems for yourself and others around you. You could end up pursuing an idea that feels amazing in the moment but isn't actually something you're truly suited for. It's vital to assess not just whether an idea excites you but whether it aligns with your natural abilities and the practical realities of the market. Passion can blind us to the bigger picture—something a trusted outsider might help us see clearly.

For example, I know a man whose wife works sixty hours a week while supporting their family. Despite her sacrifice, he continues chasing an entrepreneurial dream that's clearly not working. And despite clear evidence that his business idea isn't viable, he can't see it. His passion has turned into a costly hobby, straining both his marriage and their financial security.

The challenge here is distinguishing between a viable business opportunity and an expensive hobby. It's like seeing a ten-year-old YouTube star who becomes a millionaire and thinking, *I'll start a channel!* Or someone 6'5" deciding to become a professional basketball player simply because of their height. The odds are slim, and someone needs to step in and say, "Let's think this through."

Once you've gathered perspectives from others, conducted an honest self-assessment, and considered market realities, use the questions below to synthesize what you've learned and uncover your natural path:

- How would you describe yourself personally and professionally?
- What kind of work interests and motivates you? Why?
- What are your natural strengths and talents?
- What do others come to you for?
- What are you an unofficial expert on?
- What do people often compliment you about or say you're really good at?

By blending both outside feedback and personal reflection, you can uncover your natural gifts and start aligning them with your true purpose.

CHOOSING YOUR DIRECTION

When it comes to figuring out what kind of business to launch, people often fall into two categories:

1. **Too Many Ideas:** Your head overflows with possibilities, and it's hard to pick just one direction.
2. **No Clear Ideas:** You have no idea what you're passionate about and feel stuck or lost.

If you have too many ideas, consider the practice of "single-pointed focus" from yoga meditation. This discipline teaches you to concentrate on one thing with full attention and awareness, without getting distracted by outside noise or internal thoughts. When I applied this concept to my journey, I focused exclusively on building IIN. While you don't need to set aside all other interests and commitments, there's tremendous power in simplifying your life to focus intensely on your most important goal.

If you're feeling lost or unsure where to start, don't get caught up in social media and society's conflicting messages about success; these sound bites can be paralyzing because they overlook one key truth: Your path is uniquely yours. It's not about following a one-size-fits-all formula but about discovering your personal blend of purpose, skill, and sustainability. That's why it's crucial to be intentional about where you seek feedback. Opinions are easy to find, but not all are worth listening to. Clarity is more likely to emerge in moments of silence and self-reflection than when you're drowning in noise.

FINDING YOUR SWEET SPOT

When you're trying to find the right kind of hard, it helps to look for where different elements of meaningful work overlap naturally. If you've read career or personal development books, you've likely encountered the Japanese concept of *ikigai*. I won't spend much time explaining it because there are countless ways to frame it. Personally, I think of it as your sweet spot, where fulfillment meets practicality.

In essence, your sweet spot lies at the intersection of three key elements:

- What you love
- What you're good at
- What pays well

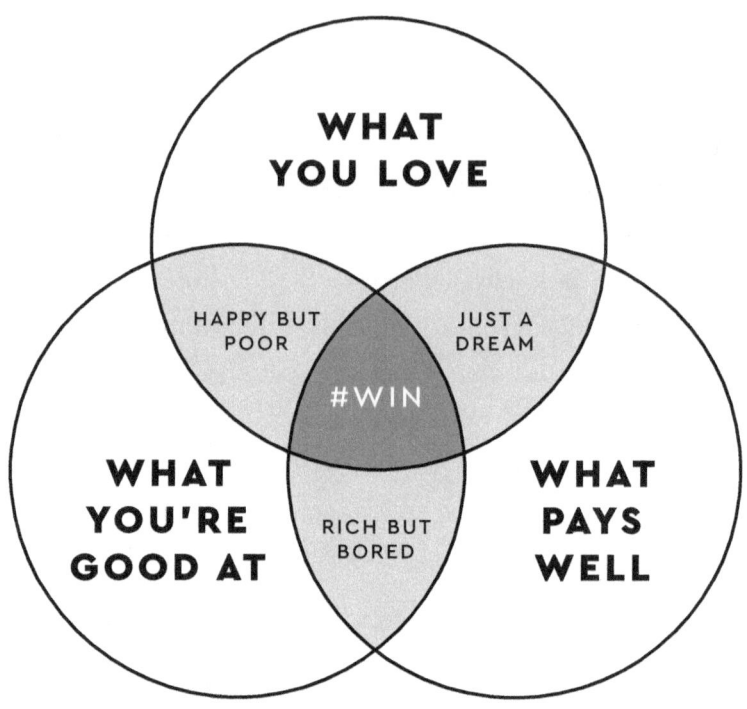

WHAT
YOU LOVE

HAPPY BUT
POOR

JUST A
DREAM

#WIN

WHAT
YOU'RE
GOOD AT

RICH BUT
BORED

WHAT
PAYS
WELL

Diagram inspired by Simon Kemp via the World Economic Forum.

When I was in my late thirties and borrowing money from my parents, I had to face some hard truths. I needed work that would both fulfill me and provide financial stability. IIN emerged from careful consideration of these three elements.

Teaching and helping others transform their lives brought me joy; it's what I love to do. I was good at breaking down complex concepts and building educational systems. And professional certification programs in health coaching could provide sustainable income because people were hungry for practical tools that empowered them to take charge of their own well-being—combining mind, body, and spirit in ways that traditional medicine often overlooked.

But finding your sweet spot isn't always easy. Sometimes, you might find work that meets one or two of these criteria but feels incomplete. Achieving your sweet spot is less about perfection and more about noticing the gaps in your current situation and adjusting along the way.

Let's explore what happens when certain elements are missing.

THE CHALLENGE OF INCOMPLETE ALIGNMENT

When your work hits only certain elements but misses others, it creates specific types of imbalances. Understanding these misalignments can help you make better decisions about your career path and business ventures.

Happy But Poor

What You Love + What You're Good At

Imagine you're doing work you love and are skilled at it—but you can't pay your bills. Take my cousin, for example. He had a real passion for crafting handmade knives. He poured his heart into it and loved every second of the work, but selling the knives wasn't bringing in enough income to support his family. He ended up living in his in-laws' basement to keep the business afloat.

Eventually, I had a difficult conversation with him: "How will you know when it's time to let this go? Why not set a timeline? If things don't improve in a year or two, you can say, 'I gave it my best shot, but now it's time to get a regular job.'" But he couldn't hear it.

This situation is particularly common in creative and healing professions. I've seen countless talented healers, artists, and coaches struggle because they haven't found a sustainable business model. Sometimes, the solution isn't abandoning your purpose but finding innovative ways to monetize it—perhaps through multiple revenue streams, through strategic partnerships, or by identifying under-served markets willing to pay for your services.

Just A Dream

What Pays Well + What You Love

Imagine having a job that pays well and involves work you love— sounds like a dream, right? But sometimes, this combination can feel more like a fantasy than reality. When your work is financially rewarding and aligned with your passions but you lack the skills or natural aptitude to excel, it can lead to frustration and stress. You might find yourself overwhelmed, struggling to meet expectations, or constantly doubting your capabilities.

For example, I once met someone who loved cooking and landed a well-paying position as a chef. But the fast-paced environment and business pressures soon wore her down. She loved the craft but wasn't prepared for the realities of running a kitchen or managing staff. Her passion alone wasn't enough to sustain the demanding role.

This mismatch can turn a dream job into a source of burnout. It's a reminder that loving what you do and earning well aren't sufficient on their own; you also need to develop the skills and confidence to thrive in that role. The good news is that skills can be learned, and with the right support and training, it's possible to grow into the job that once felt out of reach.

Rich But Bored

What You're Good At + What Pays Well

Maybe you've found work that pays well and that you're good at, but if it's not work you love, it can start to feel like you're playing a role that doesn't quite fit. Over time, this disconnect can lead to complacency or a quiet sense of dissatisfaction: You're doing good work, but it doesn't light you up.

Many people find themselves in stable, well-paying jobs that lack purpose. They're good at what they do, the paycheck is steady, but the spark is missing. While financial security matters, a career that doesn't engage your heart will eventually drain your spirit.

This longing for deeper fulfillment often drives people toward entrepreneurship; they're seeking meaning beyond just a paycheck. But before making the leap, it's wise to have a grounded plan. You might need to keep your day job while building your business on the side or find ways to make your current work more fulfilling as you explore new possibilities.

Ultimately, finding your sweet spot is a personal process of trial and error. Some people prioritize work that feeds their soul while others see a job as a practical means to an end—and both approaches are valid. By regularly reassessing where you stand, you can make intentional choices that move you closer to a work life that feels truly aligned and sustainable.

WEALTH BEYOND MONEY

Sometimes, finding your sweet spot requires completely reframing what success means to you. The hardest challenge might not be scaling up but scaling down intentionally. While many entrepreneurs chase traditional markers of success like growing their business and increasing revenue, others are questioning this paradigm entirely. Some people are consciously opting out of conventional success metrics, choosing instead to prioritize freedom and personal fulfillment over financial growth.

Consider those who choose to live simply in low-cost cities or maybe live in a trailer in the Rocky Mountains. They might earn far less than their urban counterparts yet often report greater life satisfaction. These individuals aren't failing at entrepreneurship; they're redefining it on their own terms. Their businesses might be smaller or less profitable by traditional standards, but they provide something increasingly precious: time.

In today's rushed world, time has become our scarcest resource. Many people earning substantial incomes find themselves time-poor, constantly trading their hours for dollars. This is why finding the right kind of hard means being honest about what truly matters to you. Real wealth isn't just about money in the bank; it's about having the freedom to spend your days in ways that feel meaningful. Sometimes, the toughest but most rewarding challenge is creating a business that gives you the life you actually want, not just the one that looks impressive to others.

This perspective challenges us to regularly reassess our definition of enough:

- How much money do you need to survive comfortably?
- How much do you need to earn to fund your desired lifestyle?
- What lifestyle truly brings you joy?

- How much free time do you need to feel fulfilled?
- What trade-offs are you willing to make between income and freedom?

Remember that your answers to these questions may evolve. What felt right at twenty-five might shift dramatically by thirty-five. Success isn't a fixed destination; it's a journey that requires regular reflection and adjustment as your values and priorities change.

SOLVE REAL PROBLEMS

Another aspect of finding the right kind of hard is channeling your energy toward challenges that truly matter. Once you've identified your natural gifts and sweet spot, the next step is focusing on real problems that need solving in the world.

Sometimes, what feels like a personal challenge can point to a powerful business opportunity. Take Sara Blakely, the founder of Spanx. Her journey began with a personal frustration: Existing undergarments didn't meet her needs. She wanted something comfortable, invisible under clothing, slimming, and wearable with open-toed shoes. One day, she cut the feet off a pair of pantyhose, sparking an idea that would revolutionize the shapewear industry.

In 2000, Blakely launched Spanx with $5,000 in savings. She worked days at her sales job and spent nights researching fabrics, patents, and trademarks. Her lack of fashion industry experience became an asset, allowing her to approach the problem with fresh eyes. By using her sales background to pitch directly to store buyers instead of relying on traditional advertising, she found an innovative path to market. By 2012, Spanx was valued at $1 billion, making Blakely the world's youngest female self-made billionaire.[1]

As Blakely's story demonstrates, you don't need to reinvent an industry—just start by noticing the frustrations in your own daily life. For instance, I've spent countless hours on the phone over the years dealing with terrible customer service from banks and airlines—it drives me nuts. Every time I have an awful experience, I think, *I'm here, I'm your customer, yet it feels like you're doing everything to lose me. How is this possible?* Without fail, every time, it zaps my energy and ruins my mood.

This kind of frustration isn't unique to me. There's a gap here, a need that so many people experience. If someone could create a service to streamline this process—a solution that offers effective customer support without the hassle—I'd gladly pay for it.

See? The pain points are what lead to brilliant ideas. Start by listing things that frustrate you in daily life. What problems consistently drain your time and patience? Then, prioritize the problems that

- Affect many people
- Haven't been adequately solved
- You're uniquely positioned to solve

It can help to do market research to see what industries are growing. Where is the demand? What fields are emerging that have a promising future? Look for industries where competition is low and demand is high.

1   Matt Stefon, "Sara Blakely," *Britannica Money*, April 07, 2025, https://www.britannica.com/money/Sara-Blakely.

Once you find a problem you feel motivated to help people solve, ask yourself:

- Why am I well-suited to solve this problem?
- What specific solutions can I offer?
- What insider knowledge, insights, or connections do I have that could help?
- Who am I not currently connected to who might be able to help?
- What additional resources or training might I need?

In addition to identifying problems, it's crucial to consider for whom you're solving them. The people you feel drawn to help can guide your focus and clarify your vision.

Ask yourself:

- What groups and communities do I feel strongly connected to? Why?
- Who do I feel most drawn to serve?
- When has helping someone made me really happy? What did I do and for whom?
- When helping others, what do I most enjoy bringing to them?

The key takeaway isn't just about identifying problems; it's about approaching them in unique ways. Sometimes, your lack of conventional expertise can become your biggest advantage. Just like Sara Blakely, your outsider perspective might be exactly what's needed to revolutionize an industry. Don't be afraid to question conventional wisdom or propose unconventional solutions.

VALUES AS YOUR COMPASS

Once you've identified your direction, the next step is discerning which challenges are worth tackling to build your vision. Starting a new business or scaling an existing one will present all kinds of "hard," and not all of it is productive. Your values act as a personal GPS, helping you navigate the complex terrain of entrepreneurship. They help you clarify what truly matters, making it easier to distinguish between distractions and meaningful opportunities.

Imagine you could wave a magic wand and create your ideal life, free from all constraints. What would that life look like? How would you spend your days? What would bring you the deepest joy? This vision becomes your personal compass, guiding your decisions. Should you take that leap of faith? Does this opportunity feel right? Your values help you distinguish between opportunities that truly serve your vision and those that might lead you astray. They give you the clarity to say no to projects that look good on paper but don't serve your larger mission.

To uncover the values that can guide your path, ask yourself:

- Who are my role models, and why do I admire them?
- If I could design a perfect world, what values would shape it?
- If I weren't limited by time or money, how would I spend my days?
- What achievements am I most proud of, and what values did they represent?
- What values do my closest relationships share?

To use your values as a filter for evaluating opportunities and tough decisions, ask yourself:

- Does this align with my core values?
- Will this contribute to my growth and the growth of others?
- What's the potential impact beyond just financial gain?
- How does this fit into my larger vision?
- What principles am I unwilling to compromise?

In the early days of IIN, I was teaching live classes to groups of fifty or sixty people multiple times on consecutive weekends. By 2007, after teaching the same curriculum dozens of times, I was burning out. Instead of seeing this as a setback, I listened to my core value of innovation and decided to explore online learning. This wasn't about chasing profits; I simply wanted a more sustainable way of sharing knowledge that didn't drain my energy.

The results surprised me. Moving our curriculum online caused enrollments to skyrocket from a thousand people a year to a thousand people a month. We even partnered with Apple to load our curriculum onto iPods, making learning portable and convenient. This wasn't just about using new technology; it was about staying true to our mission of making health education more accessible to everyone who needed it. We wanted education to fit seamlessly into people's lives, empowering them to grow without sacrificing balance.

When you let your values guide your choices, challenges can become opportunities for meaningful innovation.

THE WISDOM OF YOUR BODY

Just as your values can help guide your decisions, your body offers its own wisdom to steer you in the right direction. Imagine this: You're excited about launching a new business. Your passion is there, the idea solves a real problem, and it aligns perfectly with your values. Things are looking promising. Then, someone approaches you with a partnership opportunity. On one hand, they're eager and well-respected in your community; jumping on this could be a smart move. On the other hand, a part of you wants to stay focused on growing the business solo, at least until it reaches a certain level. So what do you do?

When faced with decisions like this, it's easy to get stuck in your head, analyzing the pros and cons or seeking advice from others. But sometimes, the answers aren't in your mind. They're in your body. Your body often picks up on truths that your mind hasn't fully processed yet. Those gut feelings, subtle tensions, or bursts of energy are all clues guiding you toward the right choice.

When you're on the right path, you'll likely experience

Physical Signs of Alignment:

- A quickened heartbeat from excitement, not anxiety
- Butterflies in your stomach that feel like anticipation rather than dread
- A surge of energy, even when physically tired
- A sense of lightness despite taking on hard challenges
- Deep, restful sleep despite busy days
- Natural rhythms in your work and rest cycles
- Physical resilience when facing obstacles

Positive Behavioral Signs:

- Waking up feeling driven and motivated
- Experiencing deep fulfillment from pushing yourself
- Seeing clear connections between your efforts and values
- Entering a flow state when time flies by
- Natural prioritization of important tasks
- Ability to maintain focus for extended periods
- Genuine enthusiasm for sharing your work with others

Conversely, pay attention to warning signs that might indicate you're on the wrong path.

Physical Warning Signs:

- Persistent dread or anxiety
- Tension headaches or jaw clenching
- Disrupted sleep patterns
- A heavy feeling in your chest or shoulders
- Frequent illness or lowered immunity
- Digestive issues that worsen with stress
- Chronic fatigue that rest doesn't cure

Concerning Behavioral Signs:

- Procrastinating more often than usual
- Feeling drained rather than accomplished after work
- Struggling to see how your efforts connect to your goals

- Experiencing relief when you think about quitting
- Avoiding conversations about your work
- Making excuses instead of taking action
- Consistently choosing distraction over focus

These signals aren't just random feelings; they're your body's wisdom guiding you toward or away from certain paths. Learning to interpret and trust these signals can help you make better decisions about your business and life direction.

THE BIG ROCKS FIRST

Okay, now let's zoom out to consider the bigger picture of your life. The right kind of hard isn't just about your work—it's about how your career and personal life fit together. To illustrate this balance, I like to use one of my favorite tools which I call the mason jar demonstration. Imagine you have a jar, some big rocks, and a bunch of small pebbles. If you start by putting in all the pebbles (your daily tasks and minor obligations), you'll never fit in the big rocks (your major life goals and priorities). But if you put the big rocks in first, the pebbles naturally fill in around them.

This demonstration illustrates the importance of getting clear on what truly matters to you—in both your career and your personal life. When you prioritize what's most important to you first, other things tend to fall into place around it.

Even if your current work doesn't perfectly align with your deepest passions, it might still serve your big rocks in meaningful ways. Perhaps your job provides the financial stability that allows you to support loved ones or gives you the flexibility to pursue writing, travel, or other dreams outside of work hours. This isn't settling; it's strategic. By consciously choosing work that supports what matters most to you, you're creating a foundation from which your bigger dreams can eventually take flight. The path to meaningful work isn't always a straight line; sometimes, it's a thoughtful journey where each step brings you closer to full alignment.

To identify your big rocks, ask yourself:

- What would I regret not doing if my time were limited?
- What relationships need more investment?
- What personal growth areas keep calling to me?
- What impact do I want to have on others?
- What parts of my health need attention?

Remember that big rocks can change over time. What's important in one phase of life might become less important in another. You'll have to regularly assess and adjust your priorities as your life evolves.

BALANCING CAREER AND LIFE PRIORITIES

As you clarify your priorities, it's worth considering this: Entrepreneurship can be all-consuming. It's easy to get so focused on building a business that other important aspects of life—like relationships, personal well-being, creative pursuits, and starting a family—take a back seat. While everyone's priorities differ, balancing business ambitions with the rest of what makes life meaningful can be challenging, especially when you're just starting out.

Building a business is like raising a child: It requires constant attention, ongoing nurturing, and a lot of guesswork. That's why it's crucial to be honest about your life circumstances and priorities before deciding to pursue entrepreneurship full-time. Career success is rewarding, but it shouldn't come at the expense of everything else that matters to you.

When talking with aspiring entrepreneurs, I often ask about their broader life goals beyond business success. Many are surprised by this line of questioning, but it's important. Building a business while honoring significant personal commitments—whether that's raising a family, caring for aging parents, or pursuing other meaningful life priorities—often creates a complex balancing act.

It's not that you can't pursue entrepreneurship alongside these important commitments, but you'll need to be mindful of how they intersect. Being honest about your current life circumstances and priorities will help you create a business model that complements rather than competes with them. Sometimes, this might mean adjusting your timeline, scaling back your initial ambitions, or structuring your business differently than you first imagined.

I don't share this to discourage you from pursuing your dreams but to encourage honest reflection. I've seen many people pour everything into their businesses only to wake up one day and realize they've missed out on other parts of life. There's nothing wrong with being career-driven, but it's worth ensuring that your career aligns with your broader life goals.

My own path involved prioritizing career over family. For many years, I was so immersed in my work that I wasn't interested in dating or marriage. After enough failed relationships, I saw dating as an obstacle course—one that always seemed to blow up. My career, on the other hand, felt like a challenge I could control. It was rewarding and clear-cut in a way personal relationships often weren't.

But as I reached new heights professionally, I began to wonder, *What would it feel like to reach the pinnacle of my career with no family to share it with?* The truth is, I didn't think about that when I was younger. My focus was entirely on scaling my business. Honestly, I don't think I could have built what I did while balancing other priorities, such as a partner or children. It was the right decision for me, but it's not the only way.

As you plan your business, ask yourself:

- How much time can I realistically dedicate?
- What support systems do I have in place?
- How will my business impact my family (if you have or want one)?
- What boundaries need to be established?
- What timeline makes sense for my life stage?

Entrepreneurs often navigate shifting priorities as life moves through different seasons. Sometimes work takes the lead; other times, family, personal growth, or passions outside of work come to the forefront. Each path is valid; the key is to choose them intentionally, not by default. True success isn't just about professional milestones but about how well your work supports the life you want to live.

THE IMPORTANCE OF HAVING A PLAN B

Lastly, no matter what path you choose, stay flexible—and have a backup plan. While passion drives entrepreneurship forward, building a business requires both optimism and realism—the courage to pursue your vision and the foresight to prepare for obstacles.

A lot of people say you shouldn't have a Plan B—that having a backup plan means you're not fully committed to your dream. I disagree. Even the most dedicated entrepreneurs face uncertainty and setbacks. That's why having a backup plan isn't a sign of doubt; it's a mark of wisdom. It's about being strategic and responsible.

Consider the opportunity cost: If someone thinks they'll break even after five years of building a business, they often forget to account for the income they didn't earn during those five years. If they would have earned $100,000 per year working a corporate job, that's a $500,000 deficit that needs to be part of the equation.

When launching a new venture, give yourself a realistic timeline, and stick to it. Make agreements with yourself about what success looks like at different stages. Don't live in delusion. What's your cutoff point? How long are you really willing to pursue this path before making adjustments?

This is especially important as you age. When you're in your twenties or early thirties, you might be okay with being broke while pursuing your dreams. But that equation changes as you get older. What starts as no problem in your twenties can become a serious issue by forty. You don't want to wake up one day and realize you've spent decades chasing something that isn't working.

I see this often with aspiring actors who spend years waiting tables—not because it's their passion, but because it pays the bills while they chase their creative dream. They stay convinced their big break is just around the corner, and that hope keeps them stuck. In one sense, they're following half of my advice: They have a Plan B that pays the bills. What they're missing, however, is the timeline and honest assessment. Without setting clear milestones and deadlines, that side job becomes a permanent crutch rather than a strategic stepping stone. At some point, someone needs to say, "Maybe it's time to reevaluate and consider a different path." That's not giving up; it's being wise enough to adapt your dream so it continues to serve both your life and your larger vision.

———

Like most important things in life, finding the right kind of hard comes down to balance. It's about being both practical and optimistic, grounded yet willing to dream. When you align your natural gifts with real problems that need solving, let your values guide your choices, and define success on your own terms, you create work that feels meaningful and sustainable. This doesn't mean avoiding challenges or neglecting to have a practical backup plan; it means choosing challenges that help you grow while staying true to who you are. It means listening to your body's wisdom, prioritizing your big rocks first, and recognizing that wealth extends beyond money to include time and freedom. Whether you're just starting out or scaling an existing business, the goal isn't to make everything easy— it's to make the hard parts worth it.

REFLECTION QUESTIONS

1. What natural gifts do you possess that others consistently recognize in you?

2. Where does your unique sweet spot lie at the intersection of what you love, what you're good at, and what pays well?

3. If you gave yourself a specific timeline for your business venture, what milestones would mark success?

4. What physical sensations arise when you contemplate your current career direction?

5. What big rocks must you prioritize first to create a life that feels truly balanced?

3

BUILD MENTAL TOUGHNESS

In the previous chapter, we explored how to choose challenges that align with your values and goals. Now, it's time to develop the mental toughness to see those challenges through.

Not everyone is cut out for entrepreneurship. It isn't just about having a great idea or the right credentials—it's about mindset. An MBA alone won't prepare you to run a successful business. What's more useful is building up your mental endurance, and that's not something you can learn in a classroom. This is why most people prefer the stability of working for someone else rather than taking the risks of working for themselves. Entrepreneurship is for those who understand that adversity makes them stronger. There's no shortcut or magic formula to becoming mentally tough. But through consistent practice and self-awareness, you can train yourself to thrive under pressure.

You've probably heard of cold exposure—ice baths, cold plunges, and cryotherapy—which has gained popularity in recent years. Exposing your body to extreme cold temperatures is hard. But starting a business? That's even more shocking to the system. No matter how prepared you think you are, entrepreneurship will challenge you in ways you can't predict.

You might feel confident, even cocky, after a few years in business, believing you've built up tolerance for the hard stuff. Then, out of nowhere, something unexpected happens: A top employee quits without notice, or you get blindsided by a legal issue. The truth is, business—like cold exposure—is an ongoing mental challenge. You don't just toughen up once and coast.

You have to keep stepping into discomfort, again and again. This is where many aspiring entrepreneurs get stuck. They hesitate to put themselves out there—whether it's speaking in front of an audience, reaching out to local businesses that can help promote their services, or asking for a sale. They avoid the very actions that would propel their business forward because these tasks feel uncomfortable, unfamiliar, or scary. Instead, they focus on surface-level tasks that feel safer, like perfecting their Instagram page or business logo, expecting customers to naturally follow.

But growth doesn't come from avoidance; it comes from action. The reality is that things aren't meant to feel good all the time. In a world of instant gratification and constant convenience, it's easy to fall into the habit of dodging what's difficult. Yet when we avoid discomfort, we also limit our potential. Entrepreneurship requires resilience—mental, emotional, and physical.

DEVELOPING GRIT AS
A HIGHLY SENSITIVE PERSON

The term *highly sensitive person* (HSP), coined by psychologist Elaine Aron, describes individuals who process sensory and emotional information more deeply than others.[2] As an HSP myself, I've noticed that many people with this trait struggle with building grit, which can make entrepreneurship especially challenging. While our sensitivity is a gift, it can also leave us more vulnerable to overwhelm and burnout. Starting a business is demanding, and setbacks can make us wonder if we're cut out for the role. But challenges aren't a sign to quit; they're part of the process. With the right practices, we can channel our sensitivity as a strength, develop resilience, and thrive as powerful leaders.

Sensitivity can be a superpower. It brings deep insight, empathy, and creativity—but it also needs grit to turn those gifts into tangible results. I often tell aspiring entrepreneurs, "Think about doing the maximum number of sit-ups you can, and then double it without stopping." But for HSPs, this advice isn't just about pushing harder; it's about understanding how to manage emotional and sensory overload while still forging ahead. That might mean setting firmer boundaries, creating recovery time after high-energy tasks, or shifting your mindset around discomfort. Grit isn't about forcing your way through exhaustion; it's about building the capacity to keep going in a way that's sustainable for you.

---

2   Elaine N. Aron, *The Highly Sensitive Person: How to Thrive When the World Overwhelms You* (New York: Broadway Books, 1996).

CONFRONTING FEAR
AND BUILDING COURAGE

If you're a sensitive entrepreneur who thinks deeply and feels strongly, your biggest challenge isn't just finding clients or managing your finances. It's wrestling with your own fears. The same qualities that make you excellent at understanding clients' needs can sometimes keep you stuck in worry and overthinking.

Fear shows up in business in ways that are all too familiar: worrying about rejection when pitching services, hesitating to share work because of potential criticism, losing sleep over money concerns, and constantly questioning whether you have what it takes to succeed.

This fear often drives sensitive entrepreneurs to become masters at pleasing others. They say yes to projects they should say no to. They lower their prices when asked. They reshape their business based on what others think rather than following their own good judgment. Why? Because being disliked feels unbearable.

There's a book I recommend called *The Courage to Be Disliked*. It offers a simple but powerful idea: True freedom in business comes when you stop trying to make everyone happy with you. The authors put it plainly: "A person who is not afraid of being disliked will not be bothered by criticism."[3]

This doesn't mean becoming rude or ignoring helpful feedback. It means understanding a basic truth: You can't control what others think of you, but you can control your own actions and choices.

---

3   Ichiro Kishimi and Fumitake Koga, *The Courage to Be Disliked: The Japanese Phenomenon That Shows You How to Change Your Life and Achieve Real Happiness* (New York: Atria Books, 2024).

When you release the need for everyone's approval, everything changes. You make decisions based on what's actually good for your business rather than trying to appease every opinion, chase validation, or play it safe.

Here's a simple exercise I invite you to try:

EXERCISE: THREE BUSINESS DECISIONS

Think about three business decisions you've been putting off, and list them on paper. Then, be honest with yourself: Are you delaying because you truly don't know what to do or because you're afraid someone won't like your choice? Write down your answers next to each item on your list.

More often than not, fear of disapproval is what keeps us stuck. You don't need to eliminate fear to move forward—you just need practical ways to keep going in spite of it. Here are some of my favorite strategies for building resilience and grit as an HSP:

TOOLS FOR BUILDING MENTAL TOUGHNESS

1. **Separate Facts from Interpretations**: When something goes wrong, separate what actually happened from the story you're telling yourself about it. "A client didn't respond to my email" is a fact. "They think my work is terrible and I'll never succeed" is your interpretation. Recognizing the difference helps you respond to the situation instead of your fears about it.

2. **Develop a Growth Mindset**: A growth mindset isn't about positive thinking or affirmations; it's about embracing discomfort as a teacher instead of expecting things to be easy. When you view challenges as opportunities to learn and improve rather than as threats, you build the psychological foundation for success. Setbacks become temporary and surmountable, and you're able to persist until you break through.

3. **Take One Brave Step Every Day**: Courage works like a muscle: It gets stronger with regular use. Do one small brave thing every day. Send that follow-up email you've been avoiding. Quote your full price without apologizing. Share something about your business journey on social media. These small actions build your courage for bigger challenges.

4. **Practice Handling Rejection**: For sensitive people, hearing no can feel crushing. Start building your rejection tolerance in low-stakes situations. Reach out to potential clients you'd like to work with. Apply for speaking opportunities. Request testimonials from satisfied customers. Each time you survive a rejection, the next one becomes a little easier.

5. **Work Out**: Physical conditioning builds mental toughness. Pushing yourself to do one more rep—then two, then three—trains not just your body but also your brain to adapt to discomfort. Building a business requires similar discipline—putting in consistent effort, day after day, whether or not you see immediate results.

   One aspect of this is finding purpose in routine tasks, even when they aren't exciting. Just as with physical training, where you learn to appreciate the process, building a business requires committing to the journey, not just the outcome.

At IIN, I noticed this connection firsthand. Many employees were athletes and fitness enthusiasts, though I didn't fully realize it until the day there was a marathon, and it blew my mind to see how many people took off work to participate. Their dedication showed in the office too—they brought the same grit and endurance to their jobs that fueled their training.

Exercise, in my view, does more for your body than any supplement or diet. It makes your heart pump better, bringing more oxygen and nutrients to your brain. It helps you think more clearly, reduces lethargy, and promotes better sleep—all of which boost productivity and improve performance.

6. **Eat That Frog**: As an HSP, I understand the temptation to put off complex, uncomfortable tasks, thinking, *I don't want to ruin my day.* But procrastination only compounds stress and anxiety. "Eat that frog" is about tackling your most challenging, least appealing task first thing in the morning.

   It's human nature to want to eat the things that taste good before your vegetables. But by eating the frog first—whether that's making a tough phone call or replying to an email from a challenging client—you boost your productivity and prepare yourself to handle whatever obstacles come your way throughout the rest of the day.

7. **Find Your Courage Role Models**: Identify three to five people who embody the kind of courage you want to develop. These could be successful business owners you admire, historical figures, or even fictional characters. When you're facing a difficult situation, simply ask yourself, *What would [my role model] do in this situation?* This gives you access to a kind of courage that might not feel natural to you yet.

8. **Stay in Training Mode**: When I was fully running a business, I rarely unplugged. Even on vacation, I found it challenging to take a two-week break without checking my email and then shift back into high-concentration mode. It's like an Olympic athlete's training regimen: They can't take long breaks without consequences. Look at Tom Brady, who maintained his intense training schedule even during the off-season because he knew that without consistent use, his muscles would atrophy. I believe the same applies to your business mindset and mental focus.

While many people advocate for the importance of fully checking out sometimes, I've found that keeping some level of momentum is key to my success. That may not be the most popular view, and it's not a one-size-fits-all approach. Some people thrive with clear work–life boundaries, and that's perfectly valid. What matters is finding a rhythm that sustains both your business and your well-being.

To round out this list, let's dive into one last tool for mental toughness, one that has shaped my own approach more than any other: Pivot, Don't Quit.

PIVOT; DON'T QUIT:

When things get tough, a lot of people throw in the towel. But how you handle challenges is what determines whether you'll succeed or fail. I like to think of myself as a Roomba vacuum: When I hit a wall, I simply pivot and try a different direction. If I hit another wall, I pivot again. Whether it's in my professional or personal life, quitting is never my first option. Instead, I look for creative solutions and find ways to keep moving forward.

I've seen so many sensitive entrepreneurs beat themselves up when they need to adjust their approach, viewing it as a personal failure or a lack of resilience. But resilience isn't about stubbornly sticking to strategies that aren't working. The most successful entrepreneurs are experts at strategic redirection. They understand that changing direction isn't quitting; it's smart business.

This ability to adapt and persevere is ingrained in me. I believe I inherited it from my parents, who survived the Holocaust when most of their family didn't. They had to find ways to stay alive in concentration camps, and that same determination runs through me today. When I commit to something, I follow through. Most people would give up way before I'm ready to give up on something.

For example, just recently, someone told me that business regulations wouldn't allow them to move forward with a venture they wanted to pursue. I said, "Think it through, or consult a lawyer who specializes in this area to explore potential workarounds." My approach is always to encourage creative problem-solving and seek expert advice when needed. It's not about ignoring the rules; it's about finding legitimate ways to work within them. That's the key: uncovering opportunities by thinking outside the box.

There's a popular belief that if something's difficult, it isn't meant for you— that things should always flow effortlessly if they're the right fit. But as we explored in the last chapter, it's about finding the right kind of hard. The right challenges often push us to grow in exactly the ways we need.

Now that we've explored the principles of mental toughness, let's look at an entrepreneur who committed to stepping outside his comfort zone when he realized that long-term success required expanding his limits in a strategic and sustainable way.

CASE STUDY: DEVIN BURKE

As the founder of Sleep Science Academy, Devin was passionate about his business but struggled to balance it with his love for travel and outdoor activities. During one of our calls, after he excitedly shared about his latest adventure, I asked, "How's the business doing?"

"Not great," he replied. "I'm struggling with X, Y, and Z."

Concerned, I said, "Devin, you're trying to build a business that will sustain you for the rest of your life, but I see you traveling and hiking all the time. How many hours a week are you actually working?"

When he answered, "Thirty to thirty-five," it became clear that his commitment didn't match his goals.

"No boss would hire you for a job working that many hours," I told him. "Building a lasting business often requires a real commitment up front—sometimes closer to fifty hours a week."

This conversation marked a turning point for Devin. Like many entrepreneurs, he'd started his business dreaming of freedom and flexibility. But he soon realized that he would need to temporarily sacrifice some of that freedom in order to build something sustainable. Accepting that reality wasn't easy, but it was necessary for long-term success. As we discussed the difference between comfortable challenges and growth-producing ones, Devin recognized that his current approach was creating more stress than if he fully committed to his business's growth.

We also talked about his partnership with his fiancée, Sonya, who had recently joined the business. This led to deeper discussions about their future—things like family plans and how to keep the business sustainable in the long term. Our chat made Devin and Sonya realize that if kids were in their future, they'd need to start planning sooner rather than later. Once they decided that having kids was a priority—and something they wanted to happen soon—Devin hired a backup team member. This gave them both more flexibility while keeping the business running smoothly, even when they couldn't be as hands-on. Now, they're enjoying life with their beautiful baby boy.

Devin's journey highlights the importance of aligning your commitment with your goals. While maintaining work–life balance is important, the early stages of building a business often require an extra push of dedication and focus. By accepting this reality and making strategic adjustments, Devin positioned himself for long-term growth while still preserving the flexibility he valued.

You may not be building a business on the same scale as Sleep Science Academy, so your version of stepping outside your comfort zone may look different.

Still, I recommend setting a clear growth target—whether $10k or $50k—and not letting yourself become complacent until you reach it. By making strategic adjustments and setting priorities, you can create a sustainable foundation for success while staying true to your vision.

BEING IN THE ZONE

Building mental toughness isn't just about pushing through the tough moments; it's also about finding and staying in a space where challenges feel energizing, not draining. This is where the concept of flow comes in. Psychologist Mihaly Csikszentmihalyi introduced the concept after studying what makes people happiest and most engaged in their activities. Flow happens when you're so absorbed in what you're doing that everything else fades away. You're highly focused and energized because you're tackling challenges that stretch your abilities just enough—without overwhelming you.

Let's call it being in the zone. When you're in the zone, time seems to stand still. You can do this work all day long and still wake up thinking about it. It might be writing books, creating content, or speaking on stages—whatever it is, it may be your biggest gift to the world. It feels meaningful enough to keep you committed and challenging enough to hold your attention. It's like playing a video game that's addictive in the best way—engaging and stimulating, but not so frustrating that you want to throw the controller. Even after long stretches, you don't feel drained.

I felt this way when I was building the school. I was definitely in my zone of genius; I could work on it for years without feeling drained. As a cerebral person, I've always thrived on solving complex problems, like trying to figure out the best diet for human health. I get into the zone when I'm unraveling a challenging issue or idea. Over time, I've realized that the more you stretch yourself, the greater your capacity to handle complexity becomes.

Consider a friend of mine who regularly does *The New York Times* crossword puzzle (though many prefer *Wordle* now). He's incredibly skilled at it because he's done hundreds of them and recognizes the patterns. Business challenges are similar: The more you face, the better you get at finding solutions. What once felt overwhelming eventually becomes second nature, allowing you to take on bigger challenges with greater ease.

But just because you've found your zone doesn't mean it won't shift over time. What once energized you might start to feel like a burden, and new challenges may emerge that pull you in a different direction. Staying in the zone—while also knowing when to pivot or pause—requires taking good care of yourself.

SELF-CARE TO FUEL YOUR FLOW

While pushing toward your goals, it's essential to prioritize rest and recovery. Self-care isn't indulgence; it's what will sustain you in the long run.

This might seem to contradict earlier advice about working harder, like Devin's need to increase his hours. But running a business is a marathon, not a sprint. You need to work hard—really hard—but this doesn't mean working yourself to the point of burnout. Instead, it's about finding a balance that keeps your engine running smoothly.

In my book *Heal the Healer*, I share how burnout can affect wellness professionals, a lesson I learned firsthand. For decades, I poured everything into building IIN, working day and night, even on weekends. I loved what I was doing, but no one was tapping me on the shoulder saying, "Josh, you need to take better care of yourself." After thirty years of pushing through exhaustion, the consequences of neglecting self-care eventually caught up with me and hurt my health.

If you're naturally driven to help others, you know how rewarding it can feel. You might even feel like you get a boost of energy from it, but over time, it can also leave you depleted. Many of us, myself included, began helping others out of a deep sense of responsibility. Growing up with parents who had experienced unimaginable hardship, I could feel their pain and wanted to be there for them. I was always asking, "Are you okay?" or "Is there anything I can do for you?" While this desire to give can be powerful, it can make it all too easy to overlook our own needs.

It's common for givers to believe they need to be totally selfless, like Mother Teresa. But we're not Mother Teresa; we're entrepreneurs building businesses that need to last. And that requires us to stay sharp and energized.

Sometimes, our impulse to help others can even become a way of avoiding our own challenges. It's easy to get caught up in fixing other people's lives rather than facing our own struggles—whether those are present-day issues, childhood wounds, or unmet needs. This is why self-care is so critical. Taking time to slow down, breathe, and address our own needs helps us show up more fully for others.

Peak performance requires sustaining the energy and focus needed to do your best work. Professional athletes train intensely for hours each day, but they take their recovery seriously. They understand that good sleep and proper nutrition aren't optional—they're what make the intense training possible. The same goes for business. If you want to put in those focused fifty-hour weeks, like Devin, you need to take care of your mind and body.

At the very least, that means doing the basic, everyday things that keep your brain and body functioning at their best—like getting enough sleep, eating real meals (not just caffeine and energy drinks), moving your body, and taking short breaks to recharge. Find what restores you—whether it's a midday walk to clear your head, engaging in hobbies, or spending quality time with loved ones—and make it a nonnegotiable part of your routine.

In time, you'll find a rhythm that allows you to show up as your best self, not only day after day but also year after year. Prioritizing self-care isn't just beneficial; it's fundamental for fueling your passion and staying on course for the long haul.

FINDING YOUR SUPPORT NETWORK

I've learned something important over my many decades in business: Mental toughness doesn't mean facing challenges alone. In fact, isolation often undermines resilience rather than building it.

When things get tough, many entrepreneurs (especially HSPs) retreat inward. There's a tendency to think, *I need to figure this out on my own* or *I don't want to burden others with my problems.* This private reflection has value, but too much isolation magnifies fears and narrows perspective.

What's needed instead is a strategic support network of fellow business owners who understand both the practical challenges and the emotional realities of entrepreneurship. Look for people who recognize sensitivity as a strength but won't let you use it as an excuse to play small.

The right network doesn't just offer comfort; it provides perspective when you've lost sight of your capabilities. These connections become an extension of your mental toughness, helping you see options and opportunities when you're too close to a problem.

As you face each new business challenge, remember that your support network is an essential resource—not a sign of weakness but a tool for sustainable success. The relationships you build become an investment in your resilience, helping you navigate uncertainties with greater clarity and confidence than you could achieve alone.

———

Building mental toughness as a sensitive entrepreneur isn't about hardening yourself against the world; it's about developing the resilience to stay true to your vision despite obstacles. The journey of entrepreneurship will test you in ways you never anticipated, revealing both your vulnerabilities and your hidden strengths. By embracing discomfort as a teacher, establishing supportive communities, honoring your sensitivity while building your courage, and taking consistent care of your well-being, you'll develop the mental fortitude to weather any storm.

Remember that every successful business owner has faced moments of doubt and fear. What separates those who thrive from those who abandon their dreams is the willingness to keep showing up, especially when it's difficult. Your sensitivity, when paired with mental toughness, becomes your unique advantage in building a business that both sustains you and makes a meaningful impact in the world.

REFLECTION QUESTIONS

1. What fear has most held back your business growth, and which tool from this chapter could help?

2. When have you mistaken pivoting for quitting, and how might seeing it as a strategic shift change the way you view it?

3. What's one daily habit that strengthens your mental toughness and one daily habit that weakens it?

4. What does being in the zone look like in your business, and when have you felt it?

5. Who are the people in your current support network, and what additional strengths or expertise might you need to add to strengthen it?

4

WORK WITH YOUR NATURE, NOT AGAINST IT

So many of us spend years trying to squeeze ourselves into molds that don't fit. We push against our natural rhythms and tendencies, chasing societal expectations that feel out of sync with who we really are. As a result, we feel stressed, drained, or disconnected. But what if, instead of resisting our nature, we embraced it?

This chapter is about uncovering your authentic work style and turning it into your superpower—not something you have to fix or overcome.

Looking back on my own journey, I've made plenty of unconventional choices to honor who I am. These decisions weren't always easy, but they allowed me to build a life and career that felt true to me.

From the time I started working, I knew I wasn't built for a traditional desk job. Even in the 1980s, I was one of the first to buy a car phone because the idea of working from anywhere appealed to me. Later, when IIN shifted to an online school, I fully leaned into the digital nomad lifestyle. While my team worked out of our New York headquarters, I managed the school from my smartphone. It wasn't a setup that would work for everyone, but for me, it felt natural and freeing.

Relocating to the Berkshires in Massachusetts was another decision that reflected my nature. The quiet rural environment gave me the peace I needed to focus and minimize distractions. Living in alignment with your nature isn't always easy, especially in a world that glorifies hustle and speed. I've often had to remind myself to slow down and, as I like to say, follow my own speed limit.

For some people, life moves at eighty miles an hour, and they thrive on the fast pace. That's great for them. But if you're highly sensitive, like me, a slower, steadier pace might be more sustainable. My natural rhythm is more like twenty miles an hour. Sure, there are moments when I get swept up in excitement, wanting to do everything all at once, like a kid in a candy store. But I've learned that steady, intentional progress gets me further than sprinting toward every goal. In short, I'm more tortoise than hare.

For highly sensitive people, living authentically can feel like swimming against the tide. Society often labels sensitivity as a weakness, but embracing who we are is a brave and necessary act. For me, that meant living outside of New York City despite running a school in New York City. I didn't even have an office in our New York headquarters; it was my way of saying, "I'm not here, and I'm not going to be here." Even when I had to come into the city for meetings, I held them elsewhere, often in hotel lobbies, because the office environment felt overwhelming. And you, too, can design a life that fits your needs.

The first step is self-awareness. By taking the time to understand your natural tendencies, you can begin shaping your days around them—working with yourself instead of against yourself, and moving in the flow of who you are.

Let's start by uncovering your unique productivity profile. This exercise will help you identify your natural patterns and preferences so you can create a work life that feels energizing and sustainable.

YOUR PRODUCTIVITY PROFILE

Productivity isn't about doing more; it's about doing what works for you. By noticing how you naturally operate, you can create a workflow that plays to your strengths.

Start by considering these three areas:

PRODUCTIVITY PATTERNS

Your energy and focus naturally ebb and flow throughout the day. Identifying these cycles can help you structure your work for maximum effectiveness. Ask yourself:

- What time of day am I most alert and focused?
- How long can I work before needing a break?
- Which work tasks drain me, and which energize me?

- How do deadlines and pressure affect my performance?
- What distractions or habits derail my focus?
- How do I procrastinate, and why?

For instance, you might notice you have laser focus for creative work between 8:00 a.m. and 11:00 a.m. but struggle to write or brainstorm after lunch. In this case, you could prioritize content creation, strategic planning, or other high-focus tasks in the morning. Then, use afternoon hours for lower-effort tasks like email, check-ins, or administrative work.

ENVIRONMENT PREFERENCES

Your surroundings can either support or sabotage your productivity. Reflect on what helps you focus:

- Do you thrive in silence or prefer background noise?
- What type of workspace inspires you: minimalist, cozy, or eclectic?
- Do you work best alone or around others?

Creating Your Optimal Workspace

With your preferences in mind, set up an environment that supports them.

- **For Quiet Focus:** Designate a separate space away from distractions, use noise-canceling headphones, and consider working during off-hours, when others are less active.

- **For Ambient Sound:** Play instrumental music, use white noise apps, run a small fan or air purifier for consistent background noise, or work in a café during less busy hours.
- **For Visual Comfort:** Face your desk toward a calming view, incorporate natural light, keep only essential items on your desk, and add plants or artwork that energize rather than distract.
- **For Physical Comfort and Movement:** Use an ergonomic chair, adjustable desk, or under-desk treadmill. Ensure proper ventilation, and keep a light jacket or throw blanket handy for temperature changes.

Tailor these elements to match the type of work you're doing. Deep, focused work may require silence and minimal distractions while collaborative tasks or routine work might thrive in a more dynamic environment.

WORK STYLE

Finally, think about how you naturally approach tasks and time:

- Do you function better with a structured schedule or a flexible one?
- Do you prefer specific, well-defined tasks or open-ended projects?
- Are you more effective working solo or collaborating with others?
- Would you rather focus on one task at a time or juggle multiple tasks?

EXERCISE: MAP YOUR NATURAL RHYTHMS

Spend a week tracking your energy, mood, and productivity. When do you feel most creative, focused, or drained? Look for patterns; these insights are your guide to aligning work with your natural rhythms.

By paying attention to how you naturally operate, you lay the groundwork for working smarter, not harder. In the next section, we'll dive into how to leverage this knowledge to build systems that amplify your strengths, minimize friction, and move you toward your goals with greater ease.

WORK SMARTER, NOT HARDER

You've likely heard the phrase *work smarter, not harder* countless times, but what does it really mean in practice? It's not about cutting corners; it's about being intentional with your time and energy. Hard work may get you far, but smart work sustains success.

Too often I've seen entrepreneurs push themselves to the brink of burnout by pouring more hours into a problem when what they should have done is adopt a better strategy. It's like trying to chop down a tree with a dull ax: Sometimes, the smartest move is to pause and sharpen your tools.

As Peter Drucker said, "There is nothing so useless as doing efficiently that which should not be done at all."[4] Before diving into any new task or project, ask yourself, *Is this necessary? Is this the best use of my time and resources? Is there a simpler way to achieve the same result?*

Here are my top tips for maximizing your effectiveness while avoiding burnout:

KNOW YOUR PRIME TIME

To work smarter, you need to know yourself well—starting with the times of day when your mind is the sharpest. For most people, this is first thing in the morning, when their brain is fresh and well rested. Instead of immediately checking social media or responding to emails, try reserving this high-energy time for your most challenging tasks. Others may experience a productivity boost late at night—what Chinese medicine calls liver energy time, around 10:00 p.m., when they get a second wind.

Identify your peak energy periods—as well as your slower ones—and adjust your schedule accordingly.

- **High Energy:** Tackle deep work, problem-solving, and creative projects.
- **Medium Energy:** Focus on meetings, routine tasks, or emails.
- **Low Energy:** Handle administrative work or simple errands.

---

4   Peter F. Drucker, *The Effective Executive* (Harper & Row, 1967).

A sample schedule might look like this:

- **8:00 a.m. to 10:00 a.m.:** Deep work (most alert)
- **10:00 a.m. to 12:00 p.m.:** Meetings or calls (still fresh)
- **12:00 p.m. to 1:00 p.m.:** Lunch break (recharge)
- **1:00 p.m. to 3:00 p.m.:** Routine tasks (natural dip)
- **3:00 p.m. to 5:00 p.m.:** Planning and wrap-up (as energy returns)

PRIORITIZE WITH THE EISENHOWER MATRIX

Not everything on your to-do list is equally important. Use the Eisenhower Matrix to focus on what truly matters by categorizing tasks based on urgency and importance.

To use this method, divide your tasks into four categories:

- **Important and Urgent:** High-impact tasks with tight deadlines. These require immediate attention.
- **Important but Not Urgent:** High-value tasks without immediate deadlines, such as long-term projects and growth initiatives.
- **Urgent but Not Important:** Tasks with short deadlines but little impact, often distracting from more meaningful work. Delegate these when possible.
- **Not Important and Not Urgent:** Tasks with little value and no urgency. Eliminate or avoid entirely.

Resist the temptation to prioritize urgency over importance. Quick wins may feel satisfying, but they can divert energy from more meaningful work. Use this matrix to stay on track with tasks that truly drive results.

ELIMINATE DISTRACTIONS

Deep focus beats multitasking every time. Set yourself up for success by minimizing distractions:

- Use tools like Freedom or Cold Turkey to block distracting apps or websites.
- Silence your phone or enable Do Not Disturb mode during focused work periods.
- Communicate your schedule to others in your space, and request minimal interruptions unless necessary.
- Choose a work environment that supports your productivity, whether it's a quiet home office, a library, or a coffee shop.

LEVERAGE TECHNOLOGY WISELY

Harness technology to boost your productivity. Look for tools and software that can automate repetitive tasks or streamline workflows—but avoid getting sidetracked by every new app or gadget that comes your way. Instead, only adopt tools that align with your specific needs and genuinely improve your efficiency.

DELEGATE, DELEGATE, DELEGATE

Your time is your most valuable asset as a business owner. Rather than trying to do everything yourself, identify tasks that others can handle at least 80 percent as well as you can, and delegate them. This frees you up to focus on activities that require your unique skills and vision.

Smart entrepreneurs recognize and accept their limitations. They assess themselves honestly and build teams whose strengths complement their weaknesses. For instance, I wouldn't be able to manage multiple businesses without the support of an accountant and a lawyer. I could not possibly learn everything I'd need to learn to take on these roles myself, nor would I want to. Instead, I concentrate on what I do best while letting others handle the tasks I have little interest in.

Whether it's marketing, finance, or operations, bringing in skilled professionals to handle specialized tasks is a worthwhile investment. Not only does it save you time and frustration, but it also ensures every part of your business receives expert attention.

EXERCISE: ENERGIZING VERSUS DEPLETING TASKS

Make a list of the roles and responsibilities involved in running your business. Mark tasks you enjoy or feel skilled at and those you prefer to delegate. Recognize patterns in what energizes you versus what drains you. This insight can guide how you build your team and systems.

MEASURE WHAT MATTERS (AND ADJUST ACCORDINGLY)

Define success with clear, measurable goals. Focus on metrics that reflect real progress toward your most important objectives. And as you observe these metrics over time, continuously adjust your approach to keep your business running as efficiently as possible. Remember: It's not about doing more; it's about achieving results that feel meaningful to you.

When you approach your tasks with intention and strategy, you protect yourself from burnout and lay the foundation for long-term success. These aren't just modern productivity hacks—they echo timeless ideas of balance and alignment. In the next section, we'll explore how Eastern wisdom offers another lens for understanding and honoring your nature.

EASTERN WISDOM FOR WORKING WITH YOUR NATURE

Ancient Eastern philosophies offer profound insights into living and working in harmony with our natural tendencies. These time-tested principles provide a refreshing alternative to the hustle culture many of us are steeped in, reminding us that there's immense power in alignment and flow.

Let's look at how these ideas can inspire our modern work lives.

THE TAO OF BUSINESS FLOW

In Taoism, the concept of *wu-wei* teaches us about effortless action—not through laziness or inaction, but through aligning ourselves with the natural flow of life. Think of it like swimming with the current instead of against it. When we force ourselves to work in ways that contradict our nature, we create resistance and exhaustion. But when we align our work with our natural rhythms, we find a state of flow that makes work feel easier and more fulfilling.

For example, if you're naturally analytical, don't force yourself to make quick, intuitive decisions just because that's what other entrepreneurs do. Instead, honor your need to process information thoroughly. Create systems that give you time to analyze before making important choices. Likewise, if you're highly creative, give yourself unstructured space for ideas to emerge rather than boxing yourself into rigid routines.

BUDDHIST MINDFULNESS IN WORK

Buddhism emphasizes mindful attention and the value of being present. Rather than multitasking or rushing through your to-do list, you might find more ease and effectiveness by incorporating practices such as

- Single-tasking with focused attention
- Taking regular breaks to recharge
- Creating mindful transitions between tasks

The principles of Eastern wisdom remind us to work with our nature rather than against it, creating alignment and ease in our daily lives. But alignment isn't just about how we work; it's also about who we are. Your traits, experiences, and perspective are the raw material for a business that feels authentic and connects with those it's meant to serve.

LEVERAGE YOUR UNIQUE TRAITS AND DIFFERENCES

Whether it's overcoming personal challenges, drawing from your cultural background, or thinking and interacting with the world in your unique way, your individuality is a powerful asset for connecting with others and creating meaningful solutions.

Recognizing the value of these traits will not only help define your entrepreneurial path but also shape the opportunities you can offer. By embracing what makes you different, you can create a business that resonates deeply with those who share similar experiences or needs.

Here are some examples of how to turn your unique qualities into business opportunities:

- **Living with a Chronic Health Condition:** If you face a chronic health challenge, your personal experience offers you empathy and insight that can help you connect with and support others dealing with similar challenges. You could create specialized programs, support groups, or resources tailored to people who share these needs.

- **Being Multilingual:** If English is your second language, you could leverage your multilingual abilities to serve diverse audiences. This could include offering translation services, language tutoring, or bilingual marketing, helping businesses and individuals bridge communication gaps in a global market.

- **Parenting Experience:** As a parent, you might develop products or services that address common parenting challenges. Your firsthand experience can guide you in creating solutions that make life easier for other parents.
- **Overcoming Hardships:** If you've overcome significant personal challenges, your resilience can inspire others. By sharing your story, whether through public speaking, writing, or leading support groups, you can offer hope and motivation to those who are navigating similar hardships.

Beyond these examples, there are many other ways you can turn your unique qualities into valuable business opportunities.

NEURODIVERSITY AS AN ADVANTAGE

Do you think about or process information in ways that differ from the mainstream? Whether it's ADHD, autism, dyslexia, or other neurological differences, these traits can bring valuable strengths to the table.

- **ADHD:** If you have ADHD, you might be especially adept at spotting patterns or diving deeply into subjects that fascinate you. These strengths could lead to innovative approaches or specialized solutions in your business.
- **Autism:** Many individuals on the autism spectrum excel at focusing on details or thinking through problems systematically. This ability can help you build businesses that are precise, organized, and effective in addressing specific challenges.

- **Dyslexia:** People with dyslexia often develop unique, creative approaches to understanding information and problem-solving. These skills could help you create solutions that are particularly effective in complex or unconventional situations.

The way you process information can open up fresh ideas and new approaches to problem-solving. When you lean into your own wiring, you're more likely to create products or services that genuinely resonate with people who experience the world like you do.

CULTURAL BRIDGE BUILDING

Your multicultural or immigrant background can be a valuable asset in today's global marketplace. With a deep understanding of different cultures, you can create products, services, or content that cater to diverse audiences, bridge cultural gaps, and address the specific needs of people from various backgrounds. This could involve offering products that celebrate different traditions, consulting with businesses on how to connect with diverse communities, or developing services that cater to people who are navigating cross-cultural experiences. Your unique perspective allows you to tap into underserved markets and help others navigate the complexities of cultural differences.

AGE AS AN ADVANTAGE

Whether you're just starting your business journey or you're a seasoned entrepreneur, your age and life stage provide valuable perspectives that can guide your approach.

- **Younger Entrepreneurs:** Younger individuals often spot emerging trends and understand the needs of the digital generation. Your understanding of technology, social media, and online platforms can be a huge asset as you design solutions for a younger demographic.

- **Older Entrepreneurs:** With more life experience, older entrepreneurs are often in a better position to identify opportunities to serve their own peer group. You might recognize needs within your demographic that others overlook, from healthcare services to lifestyle products.

Whatever your age, the key is to view it as an advantage—not a limitation. It gives you insights into the people you serve, helping you design products and services that truly meet their needs.

GEOGRAPHICAL INSIGHT

Where you live—whether in a city, the countryside, or on the move as a digital nomad—can shape your business offerings. As an entrepreneur, your understanding of your environment, lifestyle, and challenges can help you create products or services that cater to the specific needs of your community. If you're in a rural area, for example, you might focus on creating virtual services or resources for people who are geographically isolated. In urban settings, you may design solutions that address the fast-paced demands of city living. And if you're a digital nomad, you might develop offerings that help others navigate the challenges of a constantly shifting lifestyle, such as resources for managing remote work or maintaining balance while frequently moving. No matter where you are, you can leverage your location to provide specialized solutions that resonate with the people around you.

THE SENSITIVE ENTREPRENEUR'S ADVANTAGE

Now that we've explored how to harness your unique traits and experiences in your business, let's return to a common thread among many readers of this book: a highly sensitive nature.

For years, I've noticed something interesting about many of the most successful graduates from IIN: They often describe themselves as highly sensitive. These entrepreneurs feel things deeply, notice subtle details others miss, and sometimes worry that they're too sensitive for the business world. But here's what I've learned: This sensitivity, when properly understood and channeled, is actually a remarkable business advantage.

This deep awareness that sensitive people possess isn't just about emotions; it's a powerful business tool. When you process information more deeply and notice subtle patterns, you make better decisions. I've seen this play out countless times in my own business journey. While others might rush into new opportunities, my sensitivity has often helped me pause and notice small warning signs that something isn't quite right. What others might dismiss as being too cautious has actually protected me from numerous potential mistakes.

But perhaps the greatest advantage of being a sensitive entrepreneur is your ability to create deeper connections with your clients and team members. You naturally understand what people need, often before they can articulate it themselves. This isn't just about being nice; it's about building better products, providing better services, and creating better customer experiences. When you can truly empathize with your clients' challenges and aspirations, you can serve them in ways your competitors might never think of.

Of course, being sensitive in business also comes with its challenges. You might feel overwhelmed by too much stimulation, need more time to process decisions, or struggle with boundaries. I've learned to work with these traits rather than against them. For instance, I schedule quiet time between meetings to process and recharge. I've designed my workspace to minimize distracting stimuli. And I've learned to trust my intuitive hits about people and situations; they're usually right.

So I encourage you to stop seeing your sensitivity as something to overcome and start seeing it as your secret weapon. Your deep processing helps you make thorough, well-considered decisions. Your emotional awareness helps you build stronger relationships with clients and team members. Your attention to detail helps you create better products and services. Even your need for quiet reflection time can be an advantage; it's often in those quiet moments that your best ideas emerge.

I've noticed that sensitive entrepreneurs often excel at:

- Understanding what clients need, even when they struggle to express it
- Creating thoughtful, comprehensive solutions rather than quick fixes
- Building genuine, lasting relationships with clients and partners
- Noticing potential problems before they become serious issues
- Making decisions that align with their values and long-term vision

Being sensitive doesn't mean you're weak; it means you have access to deeper levels of information that others might miss. In a business world that often celebrates loud voices and quick decisions, your thoughtful, nuanced approach can be exactly what sets you apart.

THE INTROVERT'S EDGE

While sensitivity is a powerful business advantage, another trait that often complements it is introversion. Many sensitive entrepreneurs also identify as introverts, though the two traits are not the same. *Sensitivity* relates to how deeply you process information and emotions, whereas *introversion* reflects your preference for quieter, more solitary environments to recharge.

Whether you're a sensitive extrovert or a less-sensitive introvert, understanding your unique combination of traits is key to building a business that aligns with your nature. For introverted entrepreneurs, society's bias toward extroverted leadership can sometimes feel discouraging. But introversion brings a wealth of strengths that, when embraced, can become a significant edge in the entrepreneurial world:[5]

- **Greater Processing Power:** Research shows that introverts tend to have thicker gray matter in their brains, which indicates stronger processing capabilities. Our brains also show more activity, even when relaxed, suggesting we engage in deeper analysis and rational thinking compared to extroverts.

- **Intense Focus:** Introverts are capable of maintaining focus for longer periods. We often put in the solitary hours needed to truly master a skill or task. This ability to concentrate deeply is an asset in the creative and intellectual work we are drawn to.

- **Gifted through Dedication:** Around 70 percent of people considered gifted—those demonstrating exceptional intelligence or talent—are introverts. Part of it is that our preference for solitude and thoughtful reflection fosters the single-minded dedication needed to achieve great things.

- **Less Swayed by Social Pressure:** Studies show that introverts are less influenced by social pressure and more guided by their internal sense of right and wrong. In environments where conformity is emphasized, our ability to follow our own moral compass can benefit us.

- **Leadership Strengths:** Introverted leaders excel at deep listening, making them effective coaches in one-on-one settings. We tend to be more accepting of differences, creating psychologically safe environments where team members feel comfortable expressing themselves. Rather than seeking the

---

5   Friederike Fabritius, "A Neuroscientist Shares the 4 'Highly Coveted' Skills That Set Introverts Apart: 'Their Brains Work Differently,'" *CNBC*, February 10, 2023, https://www.cnbc.com/2023/02/07/neuroscientist-shares-coveted-skills-that-set-introverts-apart-their-brains-work-differently.html.

spotlight, we shine it on others, helping team members feel valued, motivated, and empowered to contribute their best work. This collaborative approach often results in proactive, creative, and resilient teams.[6]

If you're an introverted entrepreneur, nurturing your introverted nature at work can make all the difference. Allow time for solo brainstorming before bringing ideas to a group. Consider shortening meeting lengths or limiting larger gatherings to protect your energy. Give yourself permission to prioritize the communication methods that feel most comfortable for you, whether that's through email or one-on-one discussions. Most importantly, set clear boundaries to protect your time from unnecessary interruptions, ensuring you have the space to recharge and focus. By leaning into your thoughtful, independent working style, you'll create innovative solutions that only you can bring to the table.

ADAPT YOUR WORK STYLE AS YOU GROW

Understanding how you work best is an ongoing process. Your ideal work style isn't fixed; it evolves as you and your business grow. What works in one phase of your career may not serve you in another. As life shifts and your priorities change, remain open to adjusting your systems accordingly.

Build self-awareness by reading, listening to podcasts, or working with a mentor who can provide objective feedback. Surround

---

6   Adam Grant, Francesca Gino, and David A. Hofmann, "The Hidden Advantages of Quiet Bosses," *Harvard Business Review*, December 2010, https://hbr.org/2010/12/the-hidden-advantages-of-quiet-bosses.

yourself with other entrepreneurs who understand your challenges and can offer fresh perspectives.

As your business evolves, continue experimenting with different approaches to find what resonates with your current needs. There's no single right way to work, so let go of rigid formulas for success, and give yourself permission to try new things. Each adjustment you make brings you closer to a work lifestyle that authentically reflects who you are.

When you commit to building a business rooted in authenticity, it won't just be a career; it will become a fulfilling expression of your unique self.

REFLECTION QUESTIONS

1. When have you felt most energized at work, and what does that reveal about your natural work style?

2. Think about your most productive and fulfilling workdays. What conditions were present, and how can you recreate them regularly?

3. What work tasks drain your energy the most, and how can you adjust or delegate them?

4. Which of your differences or "weaknesses" could be business advantages?

5. What work norms or shoulds don't fit you, and how can you work with your natural rhythms?

5

—

SURRENDER CONTROL

"In all chaos there is a cosmos, in all disorder a secret order."

—CARL JUNG

When I started IIN, I had no formal business plan. Instead, I let myself be guided by the belief that whatever is running the universe—whether you call it God, nature, or the divine—wanted me to succeed. All I had to do was pay attention to the signs, seize the opportunities that came my way, and trust that things would work out.

I know it might sound crazy, but so much of my life has worked out this way. When I'm aligned with my purpose, all the pieces fall into place—perfect and seamless, as if some unseen force is coordinating the steps. One thing always leads to another.

You've likely experienced it before: those moments when everything just seems to click, as if the universe is working in your favor.

Maybe you crossed paths with someone who became a valuable connection at just the right time or stumbled upon an opportunity that changed the course of your life. These moments, often dismissed as coincidences, carry a deeper significance.

People who experience synchronicity regularly aren't just lucky; they're operating on a different wavelength, naturally attracting what they need into their lives. You've probably noticed someone like this and thought, *Wow, amazing things always happen to her. She's so lucky.* But luck isn't the whole story. Scientific research on positivity and attraction shows that, on a molecular level, our thoughts and actions help shape our reality.

For me, synchronicity thrives when I feel healthy, supported, loved, and aligned with my mission. It's strongest when I'm open and still, acting as a vessel for the possibilities around me. As an HSP and deep thinker, my natural tendency to reflect inward helps me tune into signals that guide my path. This natural sensitivity aligns me with synchronicity, but it's something anyone can develop. By trusting your instincts, avoiding overanalysis, and staying grounded in the present, you learn to spot the universe's opportunities when they appear—and recognize the bigger pattern they represent.

Remember in Chapter 3 when I wrote about being in the zone? Being in the flow of synchronicity is similar. When you're in flow, it feels like your life is moving effortlessly. Everything aligns, and you're filled with joy and natural energy. Like a hawk gliding through the sky, you ride the currents with ease.

In this state, you don't have to work as hard to achieve the things you value. That's because you are working in tandem with the universe, as you were meant to. If synchronicity isn't showing up in your life, it's often a sign that something is out of balance.

Synchronicity comes when we trust both our hearts and our minds in the present moment. By letting go of the ego—the judgmental, controlling voice in our heads—and staying centered in our hearts and guts, we allow life to unfold in ways more extraordinary than we could imagine. If we just get out of our own way and watch all the signs and signals, we can find the path that flows naturally forward. The universe already knows the optimal route; our job is simply to tune in and follow it.

This same approach applies to business—where synchronicity can unlock doors and lead to unexpected breakthroughs. It's not about luck; it's the result of preparing yourself, aligning your efforts, and being ready when the right opportunity presents itself. Cultivating this awareness means staying focused on your goals while being open to possibilities that arise unexpectedly. The more you practice this balance of intention and openness, the more synchronicity will work in your favor, guiding you toward outcomes that go beyond your initial vision.

FINDING BALANCE: THE MIDDLE PATH

Now, you might be thinking, *Wait a second, Joshua, I'm confused. Didn't you tell us earlier in the book to build mental toughness? Now you're saying we should just trust the universe?*

One of IIN's early CEOs had the same reaction. When I told him I didn't have a formal business plan, he was shocked. I laughed and said, "It's all about synchronicity. I just watch carefully, respond, and let things unfold."

A few months later, he came back with an insight that stuck with me. "It's not just about synchronicity," he said. "It's also about working your ass off. The more you work your ass off, the more synchronicity seems to happen. It's like you're showing the universe you're serious, and the universe responds by meeting you halfway."

That's when I realized synchronicity isn't some passive gift of fate; it's a dynamic partnership. The more I committed to my vision, the more opportunities seemed to line up in ways I couldn't have planned.

Like most things in life, it comes down to balance. You don't want to be the person who journals, makes vision boards, and recites affirmations but never takes action. Those things alone won't make your dreams materialize. But you also don't want to swing to the other extreme—working yourself into the ground, wearing grit like a badge of honor, and ignoring the signs around you.

It's like the lawyers or doctors who work eighty-hour weeks and, despite their high salaries, feel miserable. Pure grit without vision won't get you where you need to go. But pure vision without effort is equally ineffective. True success lies somewhere in the middle.

The middle path in Buddhism teaches us to avoid the extremes of both indulgence and asceticism. This wisdom is central to finding balance in life. Applied to our professional lives, it suggests we should neither become attached to our plans with rigid determination nor abandon our goals at the first sign of difficulty. Instead, we maintain a balanced awareness that allows us to see clearly when to persist and when to pivot, when to push and when to pause. This balance allows us to stay true to our vision while remaining responsive to the wisdom that often comes through unexpected channels.

What I've noticed is that there are often two distinct approaches to challenges: the Western way and the Eastern way.

The Western way typically emphasizes pushing through obstacles with determination and force—keeping your original goal firmly in mind and refusing to deviate from your chosen path. While this persistence can be valuable, it sometimes blinds us to other opportunities or signs that we might need to adjust our course.

The Eastern way, rooted in Buddhist philosophy, emphasizes awareness and adaptability. It's about pausing to reconsider when we meet resistance, staying open to alternative paths, and trusting that sometimes a redirect might lead to better outcomes than forcing our original plan. This approach is about moving forward with awareness and flexibility, recognizing when a different path might better serve our ultimate goals.

Ayurveda also emphasizes this same principle of balance, using *vata*, *pitta*, and *kapha* as metaphors for different energy states. The universe has a way of pushing us toward imbalance, but finding equilibrium—whether between your heart and head or your higher and lower instincts—is key to staying aligned.

That's why we developed the Circle of Life at IIN—a powerful visual tool for identifying imbalances across key areas of life, including relationships, career, physical activity, spirituality, creativity, finances, health, education, home environment, and social life. When these areas are in harmony, you naturally become more attuned to the subtle guidance and opportunities around you, creating the ideal conditions for synchronicity to thrive. My goal in helping to design this tool was to help people see where they might be overextending themselves in one area while neglecting another. Sometimes, external tools or feedback from others can reveal imbalances you might not see on your own.

When you're in balance, you're in the zone—like in sports. And when you're in the zone, synchronicity is way more likely to happen because you are aligned with your highest purpose. You're where, so to speak, the universe or God wants you to be.

For me, as a cerebral person, much of my personal growth has been about grounding myself in my heart and body. When you're in tune with your instincts and emotions, life starts to feel more effortless. The universe takes care of you and helps ensure you're in the right place at the right time, but only when you've done the work to meet it halfway.

THE WISDOM OF NON-STRIVING

This lesson came into sharp focus for me when I encountered the teachings of Dolano, a German-born spiritual teacher who became one of my most significant influences.

I met Dolano about ten years after founding IIN, during a period of my lifelong exploration of personal growth and development. What made her teachings so powerful was how she pulled everything together for me in a way that was clear, concise, logical, and refreshing.

"You already are where you're trying to get to," she would say with characteristic German precision. This simple statement was a refreshing break from the achievement-focused mindset that usually drives entrepreneurs. Dolano helped me see that sometimes our relentless pursuit of goals can become the very thing that blocks our clarity, effectiveness, and happiness.

She compared the body to a biocomputer—a magnificent system connected to universal energy that works perfectly when we don't interfere with it. This distinction transformed how I approached decision-making in every aspect of my life, allowing me to witness my thoughts rather than being consumed by them, especially during challenging times. Dolano taught me to access my brilliant brain when I needed help solving problems, but other than that, to allow myself to be directed from my heart and soul.

There's a tendency in many entrepreneurs to be caught in their heads, trying to figure everything out through sheer mental effort. After my time with Dolano, I found myself making decisions with more ease. I still use my analytical mind when needed, but I'm very clear that my thoughts aren't absolute reality; they're more like weather patterns passing through.

This wisdom can help us find more balance. When we release the desperate need to micromanage every outcome and instead align with what wants to emerge naturally, we often accomplish more with less strain. Instead of forcing our way forward, we learn to move with the current, making decisions from a place of clarity rather than anxiety or attachment.

The misconception is that surrender means giving up. But what I learned from Dolano is that true surrender is an active choice to step out of our own way. It's recognizing that, like the planets in their perfect orbits, we function best when we align with natural rhythms rather than fighting against them.

For sensitive entrepreneurs especially, this wisdom offers a refuge from pressure and burnout. It invites us to consider that effectiveness might come not from adding more effort, but from removing the obstacles—primarily our own attachment to controlling exactly how things unfold. This perspective becomes especially valuable when facing the inevitable challenges and problems that arise in business.

PROBLEMS AS OPPORTUNITIES

Recently, while living in Japan, I faced unexpected challenges with my visa status. Instead of seeing these obstacles as purely negative, I asked myself, *What's the angle here that makes this a good thing?* When problems arise, I've learned to pause and consider whether I should keep pushing forward or redirect my energy.

This approach to decision-making isn't about rushing to quick solutions. Instead, it's about staying open to possibilities and paying attention to the signs around us. Sometimes, what appears to be blocking our path is actually guiding us toward a better direction— if we're willing to notice and respond.

In the back of my head, I found myself thinking, *If I'm not meant to be in Japan, where should I be? What should I be doing?* There's power in resisting the urge for quick closure. Slow decision-making allows space for wisdom to emerge.

One practice that has helped me navigate this balance is a simple mantra: "Perfect. Perfect. Perfect." When faced with obstacles or setbacks, I pause and repeat these words, reminding myself that everything happening might be exactly what needs to happen for my growth or success. This isn't about blind optimism; it's about creating space to see beyond our initial reactions and recognize potential opportunities in our challenges.

Instead of immediately pushing back against obstacles, we can pause to ask, "What if this apparent setback is actually setting me up for something better? What might I learn or discover by taking a different approach?" This helps shift our perspective from resistance to receptivity.

The next time you're facing a business setback, rather than immediately launching into problem-solving mode, try pausing and saying, "Perfect. Perfect. Perfect." This creates space to see the situation more clearly and often reveals alternative approaches or hidden opportunities. It's not about accepting defeat; it's about staying open to the possibility that the universe might be orchestrating something better than what you originally planned.

This openness is the essence of synchronicity—the ease of being in sync with yourself and the world. But there's a flip side: when we grip too tightly, ignore the signals, or try to force outcomes, we slip into what I call reverse serendipity.

REVERSE SERENDIPITY

Reverse serendipity is that frustrating state that occurs when you're out of sync with yourself and the universe and everything feels harder than it should. You put in endless effort and still wonder why you're not making progress. Relationships feel strained, opportunities slip away, and even small tasks seem like uphill battles.

Reverse serendipity can be triggered by outside forces—like neglecting your health or staying in a toxic job or relationship—but it can also stem from within. Maybe you've lost touch with your instincts or allowed outside voices to override your own. When you're disconnected from your inner guidance, it's easy to slip into misalignment without realizing it.

What makes reverse serendipity tricky is that it doesn't always show up in obvious ways. It can disguise itself as persistence, dedication, or the belief that if you just push harder, things will turn around. You might tell yourself it's just a rough patch. But if you ignore the signs for too long, the universe tends to make them louder—sometimes in ways you can't ignore.

When you're deeply out of alignment, life has a way of throwing up roadblocks. Instead of being in the right place at the right time, you find yourself in the wrong place at the worst moment. A friend of mine was once literally shot just for being in the wrong spot at the wrong time. That's an extreme example, but I've seen plenty of smaller anti-synchronicities when the universe seems to be waving a giant red flag.

Take my cousin, for example. You might remember from Chapter 2 that he makes handmade knives. Well, there's more to that story. When I suggested he consider a backup plan to bring in more income for his family, he resisted, clinging to every small glimmer of hope to keep going, like when a famous chef bought one of his knives—that fueled months of optimism, even though it was the only sale he made that month. Then, a few months ago, while working on a knife, he accidentally stabbed himself in the stomach and had to be rushed to the hospital. He was okay, thank goodness, but it seemed like the universe was sending a loud and clear message. I wanted to ask his wife, "You think that's a sign?" but couldn't bring myself to say it. Instead, I mentioned it to her brother, who immediately said, "Yeah, I was thinking the same thing. If that's not a sign, I don't know what is."

The tricky part is that major obstacles can mean different things.

Sometimes they make us stronger; other times, they signal we've drifted out of alignment. So how do you tell the difference? It often comes down to awareness—asking whether the challenge is stretching you in healthy ways, supporting those you care about, or simply draining you. Still, many of us get so attached to a dream that we lose sight of reality, or we fall into the sunk cost fallacy—believing that because we've invested so much, walking away is impossible, even when the writing is on the wall.

This trap is especially dangerous for solo entrepreneurs. When you're working in isolation without a lot of outside input, you can get caught in an echo chamber, running on adrenaline and blind optimism. I see this all the time. Someone comes to me for business advice, wondering whether they should keep pushing forward to keep their struggling venture afloat. I cut straight to the basics and ask, "How much did you make last year?" When they hesitate and give me a lowball number like $5,000, my response is simple: "That's probably a sign it's time to pivot." Starting a business is exhilarating, but it's easy to miss the warning signs when you're out on a limb, about to fall.

That's why having trusted people who can give you outside perspectives is crucial—people who aren't afraid to say, "Yeah, that knife stabbing is a pretty strong signal, my friend." A mentor, a coach, or an honest friend can act as a mirror, helping you see what you might be too close to recognize.

This is why, while I support chasing your dreams, I also believe in having a backup plan. If your dream isn't taking off, a second option can mean the difference between struggle and stability. It also helps to be realistic about your industry, and this might require researching the odds of success in your chosen field. If the chances are slim—like becoming a pro athlete or a household-name musician—you may need to rethink your approach or build additional income streams into your plan.

To avoid falling into reverse serendipity, you also need to get clear on your big rocks—the things that matter most, as I mentioned in Chapter 2. Do you want kids? A home? A certain lifestyle? Too often, people put more effort into planning a vacation than into planning their lives, spending hours researching flights and itineraries while neglecting to map out their long-term goals.

When you're not clear on what truly matters, you risk chasing the wrong things—pushing forward simply because you started, not because it's the right path. But when you step back, reassess, and make intentional choices, you shift from struggling against the current to moving with it. That's when things start to fall into place.

RELEASING CONTROL

One of the most draining ways we resist surrender is by trying to control what isn't ours to control—whether that's other people or our own pursuit of perfection. For sensitive strivers, this tendency runs deep. We see someone struggling and think, *If I just work harder, care more, or say exactly the right thing, I can fix their situation.* Or we look at our own work and think, *If I can just perfect my website, then I'll be ready to move forward.*

This drive often comes from a noble place: a desire to make a meaningful impact and give your best to everything you do. Many thoughtful, caring, and conscientious empaths—and especially helping professionals—fall into this pattern of over-functioning, which therapists might call codependency. We become so focused on others' needs that we sometimes forget where their journey ends and ours begins. The result is pouring endless energy into trying to orchestrate perfect outcomes—for our clients, our work, or ourselves—which creates unnecessary pressure and prevents progress.

I've seen this play out countless times with health coaches. They take their clients' setbacks personally, lose sleep wondering what more they could do, or feel responsible when someone doesn't follow through with their recommendations. Some even try to force transformation by overpreparing or overexplaining, which rarely works.

The perfectionism trap works the same way. It gives the illusion of control while actually keeping us stuck. We tell ourselves that if we plan everything perfectly or polish endlessly, we'll guarantee success. But this quest for perfection often leads to

- Delaying action while waiting to feel ready
- Avoiding risks for fear of making mistakes
- Overpolishing details that don't truly matter
- Exhausting ourselves trying to control every variable
- Missing opportunities while waiting for "perfect" conditions

Here's the truth: We can't want someone's healing more than they want it themselves, and we can't control every aspect of our own path to success. What we can control is

- Our actions and responses

- The boundaries we set
- The values we uphold
- The effort we put into our work
- How we care for ourselves

For sensitive strivers, releasing control can feel especially challenging. The impulse to plan meticulously and avoid mistakes can be overwhelming. The same drive for excellence that makes you great at what you do can also leave little room for ease, spontaneity, or trust. But releasing control doesn't mean lowering your standards or abandoning your ambitions. Instead, it means

- Accepting that done is better than perfect
- Trusting that you can adapt to whatever comes your way
- Allowing others their own journey
- Giving yourself permission to take imperfect action
- Recognizing that you are already enough, even when everything isn't perfect

This shift—from trying to control everything to focusing on what truly matters—isn't always easy, but it's incredibly liberating. When we stop trying to manage everyone else's journey and our own path to perfection, we have more energy for genuine growth. We can show up fully for others while remembering that their choices and outcomes belong to them. And we can pursue excellence without getting stuck. Perfectionists often think they must get everything right before moving forward. But what if moving forward is exactly what's needed to grow, learn, and refine?

Releasing control can take many forms. It might mean saying, "This is good enough for now" and allowing your work to enter the world, trusting it will evolve over time. It could involve delegating tasks, even if they aren't done exactly as you would do them, to free up energy for what's most important. Or it might look like stepping away when your mind or body signals the need for rest, even when there's more you think you should accomplish.

Try asking yourself, *What if this works out better than I imagined?* instead of *What if everything goes wrong?* Notice when striving tips into overthinking, overworking, or overcontrolling. Then, pause. Breathe. Recalibrate. Sometimes, that simple reset is all it takes to realign with what truly matters.

And practice releasing control outside your professional life too. Whether it's family members making choices you disagree with, partners you wish would change, or world events that unsettle you, it's easy to waste precious energy on what isn't yours to manage. True peace comes from accepting what is while focusing your efforts where they can actually make a difference. In that release, surrender becomes an act of kindness toward yourself—and an opening for unexpected magic to unfold, the kind that only appears when we stop orchestrating every detail and trust the process.

CONTACT IMPROVISATION

I like to compare my approach to business to contact improvisation, a free-flowing style of dance I used to teach years ago. Rooted in Japanese Aikido—a martial art that emphasizes flow over force—contact improvisation has no set choreography, music, or rhythm.

Instead, movement emerges organically through connection—with the people around you, the space, and the energy of the moment. It's a practice of intuition, trust, and presence, in which you learn to let go and move with what arises.

I first studied contact improvisation at Smith College in Northampton, Massachusetts, and continued after moving to New York City. I was captivated by how effortlessly dancers glided through space, responding to each other in real time without any prior rehearsal.

When I began teaching live classes, I incorporated contact improvisation to help students become more open and attuned to the people and energy around them. Once you learn to navigate movement in this way, it's not hard to apply the same principles to daily life—especially to business. What may seem like chaos or randomness often reveals itself as a pattern when you pay close enough attention.

The power of contact improvisation lies in how it shifts you out of your head and into your body. You learn to release control while staying fully engaged, working with physics and gravity rather than against them. It's also a lesson in humility—when we explore, experiment, and play, we inevitably fall, slide, and tumble. But in the process, we develop deep listening skills, tuning in to the instincts of both ourselves and others.

When we stop trying to choreograph every step, we create space for unexpected moments of harmony. We open ourselves to a natural flow—one that often leads to something more authentic and beautiful than anything we could have planned alone.

THE FLYING TRAPEZE

There's a parable by Danaan Parry called "The Flying Trapeze" that perfectly captures what it means to surrender control and trust the process. In the parable, the narrator is swinging comfortably on a trapeze bar, enjoying the rhythm and security of the familiar. Then, he sees another trapeze bar swinging toward him, inviting him to let go of the first bar to grab hold of the next.

In that terrifying moment between letting go and catching the new bar, there is nothing solid to hold on to. Suspended in mid-air, he feels vulnerable, scared, and uncertain. Yet it is in that very moment of surrender—trusting he will catch the next bar—that transformation happens.

Many people avoid the void—the space between where you are and where you want to be. This in-between space can feel empty, uncertain, and a little scary, like the moment between trapeze bars. It's tempting to cling to what's familiar rather than leap into the unknown, but avoiding this void often means staying stagnant. The flying trapeze teaches us that to evolve, we must embrace the space between. The comfort of the first bar is the illusion of control; we cling to what we know because it feels safe. But transformation doesn't happen when we stay where it's comfortable. It requires taking the leap into the unknown, trusting that the next bar will appear—even if we don't know exactly what's waiting for us. It's in this leap that synchronicity aligns life's pieces in unbelievable ways.

The key is to feel the fear and do it anyway. This doesn't mean being reckless; it means taking calculated risks while accepting that you can't control every variable. Start small if you need to, but start.

Take one step outside your comfort zone, then another. Each step builds confidence and competence, even if it doesn't feel that way in the moment. And sometimes the biggest growth comes from leaping before you feel ready at all—a truth that shaped the very beginning of my journey with IIN.

START BEFORE YOU'RE READY

When I left Toronto and moved to New York to start IIN, I didn't know what I was doing. My marriage had just ended, and I got into my Honda Civic without a clear destination in mind. Through a series of serendipitous connections—a former restaurant colleague offering her place near Ithaca, a two-week dance workshop at Smith College, and a chance meeting with a macrobiotic teacher—I found my path forward. Each step was unplanned but emerged organically from the opportunities before me.

The macrobiotic teacher offered me a place to stay and a position as his assistant when I had nowhere else to go. Then, at a macrobiotic summer camp where I taught a class on opening macrobiotic centers, I met a woman who became my partner in starting a school in New York that eventually led to the creation of IIN. Looking back, it's amazing to see how improvisational it all was—following the breadcrumbs of chance rather than executing some grand master plan.

This willingness to start before feeling ready has been crucial not just in my journey but in the success of many others I've mentored. Take Lauren, who joined my team five years ago. When I first met her, she was working long hours for minimal pay, constantly doubting her readiness for bigger challenges. Every time I asked her to take on something new—whether it was creating a new product, conducting calls independently, or managing financial responsibilities—her first response was hesitation.

But Lauren had something special: a background in competitive sports that had taught her the value of pushing through discomfort. She drew on that athletic mindset, transposing the discipline and resilience she'd learned on the field to her professional growth. Instead of waiting until she felt completely confident, she embraced the challenge and pushed through her barriers, ultimately becoming one of our most successful team members.

Also, Lauren had strong parental role models who demonstrated resilience and adaptability in the face of challenges. It's easier to take risks and push past your limits when you see your parents doing the same—when they model the kind of persistence and flexibility that becomes second nature. For many of us, these early lessons in resilience are foundational. It's much harder to adopt this mindset if your parents didn't show you how to approach life with that kind of tenacity. But if you're fortunate enough to have grown up in an environment where going after what you want, even in uncertainty, is normalized, you're more likely to embrace the unknown and leap before you're ready.

When I talk to aspiring health coaches, entrepreneurs, or really anyone pursuing a meaningful goal, I often hear the same fear: "I don't know enough; I'm not ready." They want to wait until they have more knowledge, experience, or confidence. But here's the truth: If you wait until you feel completely ready, you'll be waiting forever. This quest for perfect preparation is often just another form of resistance—a sophisticated way of procrastinating taking action.

Starting before you're ready isn't just about making things happen; it's about being willing to be imperfect at something new. Think about a child learning to walk. They don't wait until they're sure they won't fall. They stumble and fall countless times, and through that very process, they develop the strength and balance they need. This willingness to approach challenges with curiosity and openness rather than self-judgment is what psychologists call the beginner's mindset. Research shows it can actually accelerate learning and growth.

The key to starting before you're ready is developing what I call adaptive resilience—the ability to stay flexible and responsive while moving forward. It's like being a jazz musician improvising in real time, adjusting to the rhythm and changing your notes to stay in tune when things don't go as planned. Let's say you're preparing to teach your first workshop. You've meticulously planned every detail—the perfectly timed slide presentation, the handouts, the room setup. Then, on the day of the event, everything that could go wrong does: The projector dies, your handouts get mixed up, and a construction crew starts drilling right outside the window.

At that moment, you have a choice. You can either freeze up because things aren't perfect, or you can adapt and flow with the circumstances. The adaptive entrepreneur might turn the workshop into an interactive discussion, use the wall as a whiteboard, and even incorporate the construction noise into a conversation about dealing with daily stressors. This ability to pivot while maintaining your core purpose is what separates successful entrepreneurs from those who get stuck in their own expectations.

What will starting before you're ready look like for you? Maybe you dream of opening your own wellness center. Instead of waiting until you feel fully prepared, you could take a part-time job as a wellness coach at a local gym while starting small with your own practice. Don't worry about undercharging at first or making mistakes in how you structure your time. Each misstep will teach you something valuable that you can carry forward.

Readiness isn't a destination; it's a practice. Successful people don't wait until they feel ready; they take action while embracing the discomfort of uncertainty. They understand that true confidence comes not from perfect preparation but from taking imperfect action and learning as they go.

TRUST YOUR PEOPLE

Surrendering control isn't just about letting go of your own expectations; it's also about trusting the people you've chosen to work with and giving them space to excel. When you trust your team members, advisors, and collaborators, you free up mental and emotional energy to focus on what you do best. The most successful ventures are built on a foundation of trust where each person's strengths complement the others' weaknesses.

You know the term *helicopter moms*? I'm like the opposite. When I find hardworking people I trust, I let them make decisions and run with ideas. I give them autonomy because I believe in synchronicity and prefer focusing on the bigger picture. Does this mean nothing ever goes wrong? Of course not. But setbacks will happen regardless, so why waste energy trying to control every detail?

This mindset creates an environment where creativity and

innovation thrive. Trust is a partnership, not a passive act. It's saying, "I trust you to make the right decisions, and I trust that if things go wrong, we will work together to find a solution." By leaning into this trust, you create space where unexpected turns can lead to new opportunities.

SURRENDER TO LEARNING

The last point I want to make about surrendering control is one that often gets overlooked: the importance of staying open to learning. While confidence is valuable, being overly confident can become counterproductive. We all have that person in our lives—maybe a friend or family member—who's a bit of a know-it-all. You try to offer a suggestion, but they can't be told anything. They've already got it all figured out. The truth is, when you shut yourself off from learning, you also shut yourself off from growth and possibility.

Some of my biggest breakthroughs have come from simply being willing to listen to and learn from people with different perspectives from my own. When you're coachable, suddenly feedback isn't an attack; it's a gift. Challenges aren't threats; they're chances to level up.

Consider the entrepreneur who finally finds success after years of struggle, not by pushing harder at their original idea but by listening to a customer's casual comment that revealed a completely different direction—or the artist who breaks through creative blocks by studying a discipline seemingly unrelated to their craft. When we surrender to learning, we acknowledge that wisdom can come from anywhere—often from the most unexpected sources. This openness creates a fertile ground for synchronicity to flourish. By releasing our grip on being right or knowing everything, we tune into the subtle guidance that's always available to us.

HOW TO ATTRACT MORE SYNCHRONICITY INTO YOUR LIFE

So how do you put these ideas into practice in a way that invites synchronicity more often? You can't force it, but you can create the conditions for it to emerge. Here are a few practices to help you stay open, aligned, and receptive.

1. **Trust Your Gut Instinct:** Remove the analytical mind from the equation. Instead, follow your instincts.

2. **Tune into Your Body:** Pay attention to the subtle physical and emotional clues your body gives you; those inner whispers will guide you toward the next right step.

3. **Maintain Balance:** Cultivate a calm, centered presence by balancing your primary needs (food, relationships, etc.) and harmonizing your inner energies (yin and yang). You can use tools like the Circle of Life, which I mentioned earlier.

In addition, it's helpful to reflect on the synchronicity that's already occurred in your life. Start by asking yourself:

- What serendipitous events have happened to me in the past year?
- What was going on for me physically, mentally, and emotionally before those events unfolded?
- What obstacles or blocks to synchronicity have I noticed in my life?

———

Remember that surrendering control isn't about giving up; it's about opening up. When you let go of rigid expectations, you make room for new possibilities to emerge. Like contact improvisation, business and life require us to stay responsive and adaptable, to trust the process while remaining fully engaged in each moment. The universe has a way of meeting you when you take that first courageous step into the unknown. The goal isn't to eliminate uncertainty; it's to learn how to move with it.

REFLECTION QUESTIONS

1. How can you invite more synchronicity into your life moving forward?

2. What area of your life would benefit most from surrendering control right now?

3. Who are the people you need to trust more?

4. What's one step you could take today before feeling ready?

5. What anti-synchronicities or recurring challenges might you be ignoring in your life right now, and what message could the universe be trying to send you?

6

DON'T TRY TO BE LIKE EVERYONE ELSE

In this fast-paced world, it's easy to get swept up in expectations and societal norms. We're taught to fit into neat little boxes, chase external validation, and conform to others' definitions of success. Yet deep down, a persistent voice urges us to break free and discover who we truly are.

Success isn't one-size-fits-all. It's as unique as your fingerprint. Trying to squeeze into someone else's version of success is like wearing shoes two sizes too small: uncomfortable and limiting. Maybe that's why I have so often felt like a rebel, drawn to paths others warned me against.

One of the clearest examples was many years ago, when my friend Mark and I visited Sacred Falls in Hawaii—a waterfall known as the most breathtaking on the main island. Along the thirty-minute hiking trail to the falls, signs warned, "FLASH FLOOD AREA," urging visitors to evacuate immediately if it rained, as flash floods could occur suddenly in this narrow canyon. Sure enough, just five minutes after reaching the waterfall, it started raining, and everyone in the area quickly packed up to leave. Mark and I reluctantly followed, but halfway out, something stopped me.

I turned to Mark and said, "You can go. I'm turning around to go back to the falls." As I walked back against the flow of people evacuating the area, I got plenty of concerned looks. But something about this place felt sacred, otherworldly, and I couldn't leave. I craved these moments of stillness, of being at one with nature.

Alone at the base of the falls, I felt surrounded by a living presence—the rush of the water, the chorus of insects and animals, the vastness of the forest. As darkness settled in, the sounds grew sharper, layered, almost musical. That night became one of the most profound spiritual experiences of my life. I felt an overwhelming sense of connection to everything around me, as if the forest itself were awake and speaking. It changed me—and it was an experience I would have missed entirely if I hadn't trusted my inner voice.

Now, I'm not suggesting you spend a night alone in a canyon during a rainstorm. In fact, Sacred Falls State Park is now closed to hikers because of a deadly landslide in 1999. Was my decision risky? Absolutely. But the point isn't about taking physical risks; it's about trusting your intuition when it matters most. Because magic rarely happens when you're following the crowd.

Humans have a natural tendency to follow the herd. Standing out can feel intimidating, especially when our culture places so much value on belonging. But success in entrepreneurship often means learning to distinguish between unnecessary risks and calculated opportunities that others might miss because they're too busy conforming. This isn't just about business—it's about how we live.

If you're like me—someone who's always felt different—you've probably poured a lot of energy into trying to belong. I know this struggle well. Growing up in a close-knit Jewish community, I wanted nothing more than to please my parents. But deep down, I knew I didn't fit the mold, and forcing myself into it left me exhausted.

This conflict between my authentic self and societal expectations took its toll. When I was diagnosed with schizophrenia in my early twenties, a friend told me, "You have no coping mechanism to deal with reality." Looking back, I see now that I was caught between the voice of my intuition and the voice of my conditioning—a tension many people resolve by suppressing their inner truth and conforming. But I was unwilling, or unable, to do that. And when you go against the grain, society often labels you as the problem.

But here's what I learned: What others saw as a problem was actually my greatest strength. I went from being pathologized by doctors to starting the largest nutrition school in the world—not because I'm some rare breed of genius but because I was brave enough to trust my ideas even when others didn't.

The truth is, the status quo we're all trying to fit into is deeply flawed. Around the world—and especially in America—people are unhealthy, overstressed, and disconnected. Millions rely on antidepressants, sleep aids, and stress medication just to function. If this is the reality to which we're conforming, doesn't it make more sense to question the system than to bend to fit it?

THE POWER OF FITTING OUT

Living in alignment with your true nature isn't just about being different. It's about being intentionally authentic—what I call fitting out. Fitting out means being your true self unapologetically, even if it challenges conventional wisdom or industry norms.

Today, I live in the woods. I'm not married. I never had kids, and I keep only a few close friends so I can maintain my sense of freedom, inner peace, and connection to my inner self. Have people judged my lifestyle? Probably. But these weren't acts of rebellion; they were conscious choices to honor what I knew was right for me, even when that went against societal expectations.

I've seen this same spirit in my most memorable mentors and teachers, as well as in some entrepreneurs I've mentored over the years. The ones who really thrive aren't the ones following some cookie-cutter business template; they're the ones who dare to trust their instincts and create offerings that truly reflect who they are and what they believe in.

Consider pioneers like Michio Kushi, who had the courage to introduce macrobiotics to America back when most people thought eating brown rice was weird and had never heard of concepts like yin and yang. He stayed true to his vision even when people dismissed his ideas as too foreign or extreme. Or look at Werner Erhard: He transformed the personal development field by creating est (which later became the Landmark Forum). People said his methods were too unconventional, too intense, but he knew in his heart that people were ready for real transformation.

We all have a deep inner knowing, but many of us are afraid to trust it. Instead, we turn to outside influencers and so-called experts to tell us how to live. For new entrepreneurs, the pull toward outside validation can feel particularly strong. Breaking this habit takes effort, but the payoff is worth it: You'll start living life on your own terms. Your work will feel inspiring instead of draining, and when your choices align with your values, your enthusiasm and consistency naturally improve.

Now, ask yourself: How much of your intelligence and creativity have you been channeling into fitting in? What could happen if you redirected that energy into fitting out—choosing a path that truly excites you?

INNOVATION THROUGH UNCONVENTIONAL THINKING

Part of fitting out is thinking differently and challenging what's been accepted as the norm. This mindset can unlock creativity and innovation, empowering you to push boundaries in your business.

One of my favorite ways to help people break free from conventional thinking is by playfully challenging their assumptions. I call these moments brain freezes—instances where I say or do something unexpected to catch people off guard and disrupt their usual thought patterns. You could also call it punking people.

In conversations, I might throw in an unexpected observation, a strange joke, or even a nonsensical comment to shake things up. Often, the response is a polite, "Oh, okay," as if they're trying to maintain social appropriateness or pretend my comment didn't happen. My goal isn't to be inappropriate—it's to break people out of their programmed responses. When we're stuck in our routines, we miss out on opportunities for creativity and innovation.

I took inspiration for this approach from my time in India, where I studied under unorthodox spiritual teachers. Their methods were at times provocative: They used humor, playful contradictions, and unexpected actions to challenge rigid beliefs and get people to think for themselves. It wasn't random; it was a way to provoke self-reflection and awakening.

The same idea applies to business. Some of the best solutions come from stepping outside the usual way of doing things and questioning long-held assumptions. For instance, I once asked myself, *Why does someone need a degree in therapy or nutrition to offer compassionate support, accountability, and guidance for people struggling with their health—especially when so many are suffering in a broken healthcare system?* That simple question led me to create the field of health coaching.

By stepping outside the norms, you can capture people's attention and carve out a unique space in your industry. Thoughtfully challenging expectations is a powerful way to add value and stand out in a crowded market.

CARVING OUT YOUR UNIQUE SPACE IN THE MARKET

Speaking of standing out in a crowded market, I want to introduce you to a business strategy called the Blue Ocean Strategy. Think of it this way: Most businesses are swimming in crowded waters, fighting for the same customers. That's what we call a red ocean—it's exhausting and competitive. But what if you could swim somewhere new? That's your blue ocean—a space you create that's all your own, where competition doesn't matter because what you're offering is unlike anything else.[7]

For example, imagine you're at a crowded farmers' market. Every other stall is selling organic vegetables or homemade soaps. That's a red ocean—everyone's competing for the same customers, lowering their prices, and shouting louder to be heard.

Now, imagine instead that you notice there's no one offering ready-to-cook organic meal kits with recipe cards for busy parents. You've just spotted your blue ocean—a space where you're the only one swimming, offering something people need but can't find anywhere else.

This isn't about being different just to be different. It's about creating something that truly serves people in a new way. Think about your smartphone: Before the iPhone came along, phones were either super basic or so complicated that only tech-savvy people could figure them out. Apple didn't just make another phone; they redefined what a phone could be, making it intuitive and accessible to everyone. They saw a need and filled it in their own way, creating something both innovative and widely appealing.

That same principle has guided my career. I've always had a knack for spotting gaping holes in society and creating innovative solutions to fill them. When I started IIN, I saw how broken our healthcare system was. Instead of creating just another nutrition school, I asked

---

7   W. Chan Kim and Renée Mauborgne, "Blue Ocean Strategy," *Harvard Business Review*, October 2004, https://hbr.org/2004/10/blue-ocean-strategy.

myself, *What if we could teach people to understand their own unique bodies and help others do the same?* That's how bio-individuality was born—the idea that there's no one-size-fits-all approach to health. We combined nutrition education with personal growth, business skills, and coaching techniques. Suddenly, people who never saw themselves in traditional healthcare found their calling.

Later, after seeing how confusing and expensive health insurance had become in America, I co-founded Knew Health, a membership-based health-sharing community that offers an alternative to traditional health insurance. By pooling resources among members, Knew Health helps cover unexpected medical costs while promoting a proactive, wellness-focused approach to healthcare.

At the core of both of these companies is the same idea: breaking the mold, offering something new, and meeting people where they are. By paying attention to what's missing and thinking outside the box, I've been able to create solutions that actually work for people in a way the usual systems don't.

Finding your blue ocean becomes much easier when you pay attention to what's happening in the world around you. While trusting your intuition plays a role, it's just as important to recognize emerging markets that are beginning to take off. These can reveal promising opportunities where demand is high but competition remains low. Notice groups of people whose needs aren't being met or interesting ways to combine two different services—like a home organization business that integrates feng shui to improve people's sense of balance and harmony in their living spaces. Some of the best opportunities come from solving growing problems or responding to new laws and rules that change how industries work.

The key isn't just identifying what people want today but also anticipating what they'll need tomorrow by paying attention to trends and what's changing in society.

Ready to find your own blue ocean? Here's how to start:

1. **Lean into Your Sensitivity:** What frustrations do you notice that others might miss? What do your clients keep complaining about?

2. **Trust Your Gut:** Those subtle hints about what's missing in your field are often spot-on.

3. **Blend Your Talents:** Love coaching and have a knack for event planning too? Maybe you could create transformative retreats that combine both.

4. **Stay True to Yourself:** What do people naturally seek you out for? The problems you're uniquely equipped to solve could be the key to your breakthrough idea.

Remember: You don't need to fish in the same small pond as everyone else. There's a whole ocean of possibilities out there, waiting for someone exactly like you to cast your net. While it's fine to get inspired by what others are doing, focus on creating something uniquely yours—something only you can bring to the table. Your unique offering might be exactly what someone out there is searching for.

And carving a new path doesn't always require bold, dramatic moves. Sometimes, it's about starting small and experimenting in ways that feel authentic to you.

STARTING SMALL:
TESTING UNCONVENTIONAL IDEAS

Okay, take a breath. Take a moment. Let's say you've started to get clear on what you want to do, but now the big question hits: "How do I actually begin?" It's easy to feel overwhelmed by the big picture, but honoring your authentic self doesn't require making huge dramatic changes all at once. You can start by taking small intentional steps. These calculated risks will help you build momentum, gain confidence, and gather valuable feedback as you test the waters.

One way to begin is by sharing parts of your personal journey—your challenges, growth, and lessons learned—through newsletters or social media. Vulnerability can be a powerful tool in business, especially in the healing and wellness space. When people connect with your story, they'll feel a deeper connection to your work.

This approach can extend to other aspects of your business, like experimenting with how you present yourself online or wearing something that reflects your personality. Many successful entrepreneurs started with such small steps before finding their unique path.

Take IIN graduate Benjamin Camras, for example. After leaving his nine-to-five job, Benjamin set out to build an online business. As he experimented with different approaches, his focus went through several iterations before he found his niche in dating and relationship coaching. With a mix of heartfelt advice, humor, and a signature mustache, he rebranded himself as The Flirt Coach and built an engaged online community around helping people navigate the early stages of dating with confidence and authenticity. Today, Benjamin reaches a global audience through his social media following, *Flirtations* podcast, coaching services, and digital resources. His journey is a great example of how starting small, staying true to your style, and being patient with the process can lead to meaningful growth over time.

TESTING YOUR UNCONVENTIONAL IDEAS

With these initial steps building momentum, the next phase is to systematically test your ideas. Testing on a small scale not only minimizes risk but also allows you to gather insight, make adjustments, and build confidence before committing fully.

The key to successful testing is following a structured approach:

- Start with a simplified version of your offering.
- Test it with a small targeted audience.
- Gather detailed feedback.
- Refine based on insights.
- Scale gradually as you confirm what works.

Let's look at two different entrepreneurs who used this approach effectively.

Visual Health Coaching: Aisha's Story

Aisha, a health coach with a background in art therapy, wanted to incorporate visual journaling into her health coaching practice. Instead of overhauling her business overnight, she:

- Invited three interested clients to try fifteen-minute visual journaling exercises during their sessions
- Provided prompts like "Draw what energy feels like in your body after eating different foods"
- Collected feedback on how the process impacted their progress

The results were overwhelmingly positive. Aisha's clients felt more connected to their bodies and gained new awareness of their habits through the simple act of drawing their experiences. One client had a breakthrough when she drew how different foods affected her energy levels. Suddenly, she understood why she experienced afternoon fatigue and adjusted her diet accordingly. Another client started drawing her stress levels in her journal and spotted patterns she hadn't noticed before. These patterns helped her identify triggers and develop strategies to reduce anxiety.

Encouraged by this success, Aisha eventually created a full Visual Wellness Journey program that resonated deeply with her audience. Before long, she had a waiting list of clients specifically requesting her visual coaching approach.

Adaptogenic Tea Blends: Maya's Journey

Maya, an herbalist, wanted to create a line of adaptogenic teas for stress relief. Instead of diving straight into large-scale production, she:

- Developed a single tea blend and sold it in small batches to twenty clients at a discount

- Gathered feedback on taste, preparation, effects, and packaging
- Hosted focus groups to gather detailed insights

The feedback Maya received was both surprising and eye-opening, highlighting details she hadn't thought of. Many people found the tea a bit too bitter and wanted a smoother taste. Others asked for clearer preparation instructions and more information about the adaptogens—what they are and how they work. The most interesting discovery of all was that about half the group preferred drinking the tea in the morning for an energy boost while the other half liked it in the evening to relax and unwind.

Maya used this feedback to create two distinct tea blends: one to boost morning energy and another to promote evening relaxation. She refined the recipes to enhance the flavor and added detailed explanations of each ingredient's benefits to the packaging. To elevate the experience even further, she created beautiful ritual cards, transforming tea preparation into a mindful and intentional practice. Her final product was far better than her initial idea, and the thoughtful development process deepened her connection with clients, making them feel seen and valued.

Can you see from these examples why testing matters? Both Aisha and Maya avoided costly mistakes by starting small. Testing helped them refine their ideas and stand out in ways that felt fresh, authentic, and deeply aligned with their audience's needs.

EXERCISE: ONE UNCONVENTIONAL IDEA

Think of an unconventional idea you've been hesitating to pursue. What's the smallest version of this idea you could test this week? Define what success would look like for this micro-test, and take the first step.

NAVIGATING THE CHALLENGES OF FITTING OUT

As you step out of your comfort zone and bring your unique vision to life, you may encounter challenges that test your resilience, creativity, and self-trust. These are the growing pains of building a business that's authentically yours. But with the right strategies, you can move through these challenges with confidence and care. Let's explore how.

- **Financial Uncertainty:** One of the first hurdles many new entrepreneurs face is financial uncertainty, especially when they're doing something different or unconventional. It's normal to wonder if you're taking a big risk, but you can ease that worry by starting small. Keep some conventional offerings while experimenting with your innovative ones. Build up a financial cushion, and create multiple revenue streams so you aren't relying on only one. Understand that when you're introducing something new to the market, it often takes longer for people to understand and embrace it. That's okay; give yourself permission to grow slowly and sustainably.

- **Resistance from Others:** When you choose to follow your authentic path, you may face resistance from others. Family members might question your choices, industry peers may doubt your methods, and potential clients could be hesitant to try something new. This can be especially tough for sensitive entrepreneurs who may feel more affected by criticism. Find a support network of like-minded innovators, and keep a record of positive feedback and success stories from those who benefit from your work. This will help you stay grounded, focused, and connected to the value you bring.

- **Market Education:** Introducing new ideas means you may have to educate your market, which can be a slow process. It's not about convincing people right away; it's about gently guiding them to understand what you offer and why it matters. Use storytelling to connect with potential clients and make your unconventional methods more approachable. Offer low-risk ways for them to experience your work, and they'll begin to see the value.

- **Self-Doubt:** Self-doubt will inevitably crop up, especially when you're venturing into uncharted territory. On those tough days, remember why you started. Keep a journal of your wins and positive feedback to lean on when things get uncertain. Learn to distinguish between your intuition and fear. Fear might try to pull you back into your comfort zone, but intuition will guide you forward.

- **Professional Isolation:** As you build something new, it can feel lonely, but you don't have to do it alone. Connect with visionaries and innovators who understand what it's like to challenge industry norms. Seek mentors who have successfully navigated unconventional paths, and join communities specifically for creative entrepreneurs pushing boundaries in your field. These connections will provide both inspiration and practical insights for overcoming the unique obstacles that arise when you're creating something truly different.

- **Implementation Challenges:** When it comes to implementing your ideas, break them down into manageable pieces. Test things out, see what works, and be willing to adjust. Progress, not perfection, is what matters most. Every entrepreneur who's created something truly unique has faced moments of trial and error—don't let that scare you.

MANAGING VISIBILITY AND SENSITIVITY

Now, as you push boundaries, you're also going to be more visible. People will notice, and for sensitive entrepreneurs, that can feel overwhelming. Our heightened awareness of others' perceptions can make standing out especially challenging. But the key is to manage this visibility in a way that protects your energy, allowing you to show up as your authentic self without burning out.

Here are some strategies for managing increased visibility while honoring your sensitive nature:

1. Schedule specific times for high-visibility activities (like social media, networking, or client calls) when your energy is strongest.

2. Create a quiet retreat area in your office or workspace where

you can decompress between interactions. This might be a cozy corner with plants and soft lighting or a separate room.

3. Practice saying no to opportunities that don't align with your energy levels or values. Remember that every yes to something that drains you is a no to something that might energize you.

4. Set clear boundaries around your availability and response times to prevent emotional overwhelm. Consider implementing office hours for client communications.

5. Build regular sensitivity breaks into your day; even five or ten minutes of quiet time can help you reset.

6. Create morning and evening rituals that ground you. This might include journaling, meditation, movement, or time in nature before or after engaging with clients or social media.

7. Engage in quick bursts of physical activity throughout the day to release absorbed energy. Try keeping a yoga mat in your office for quick stretching sessions between calls, practicing breathwork, or taking short walks outside to clear your energy field.

8. Maintain a strong support system of people who understand your sensitive nature. This might include other HSP entrepreneurs, a mentor, or a therapist who can help you process the emotional aspects of business visibility.

AUTHENTICITY CHECKPOINT

When considering any business strategy or marketing approach, use this framework to ensure you're staying true to yourself while growing your business:

Energy Alignment Check

- Does this strategy energize me or drain me?
- Can I sustain this approach long-term without burning out?
- What modifications would make this more sustainable?

Authenticity Assessment

- Am I making this choice from authentic desire or from fear/pressure?
- Does this feel true to my values and natural way of being?
- Would I feel proud telling others about this approach?

Impact Evaluation

- How will this affect my most sensitive clients?
- Does this contribute positively to my field?
- Am I solving a real problem in a way that feels genuine?

Practical Integration

- What boundaries do I need to set to maintain authenticity?
- How can I communicate these boundaries clearly to others?
- What support do I need to implement this authentically?

Revisit this checkpoint regularly, especially when—

- Launching new offerings
- Considering new marketing strategies
- Scaling your business

- Facing pressure to conform to industry norms
- Feeling disconnected from your work

Remember: Your sensitivity isn't a liability; it's a gift that allows you to create deeper connections and more meaningful solutions for your clients. By honoring your nature while strategically pushing your comfort zone, you can build a successful business that energizes rather than depletes you.

———

As you move forward on your entrepreneurial journey, remember that you—not societal pressures or the doubts in your mind—are in control of your future. The greatest breakthroughs often come when you trust your instincts and embrace what sets you apart, whether it's your sensitivity, intuition, or fresh perspective. Stepping into your authentic self opens doors for innovation, connection, and impact that others might overlook. And when you allow yourself to be truly seen, you inspire those around you to do the same in a world where genuine, courageous authenticity is rare. Trust your differences, challenge the norms, and let your true essence lead the way; the world is waiting for what only you can offer.

REFLECTION QUESTIONS

1. What would your business look like if you stopped trying to fit in and fully embraced what sets you apart?

2. How can you put your own unique spin on the product or service you provide and increase the value you offer?

3. What frustrations or gaps do you notice in your field that others might be overlooking?

4. What is one product or service idea you could test with a small group this month?

5. Which aspects of increased visibility feel most challenging to you as a sensitive person?

7

OWN YOUR WORTH

Early in my career, I received advice that seemed counterintuitive to everything I believed. "Wear a suit," a mentor told me, "the most expensive suit you can buy." At first, I laughed it off. I had never been one to care much about appearances. But my mentor insisted, "People will judge you by what you wear, whether you like it or not." That simple piece of advice transformed not just my wardrobe but also how I carried myself as a leader and entrepreneur. While other teachers dressed casually, showing up looking polished and professional became part of my signature style. My presence commanded respect before I even spoke a word.

You see this principle play out everywhere. Think about boarding a plane. Most passengers prioritize comfort—sweatpants, hoodies, sneakers. But notice how your perception shifts when someone boards the plane in a well-tailored outfit. They stand out. They command attention. And guess what? Dressing the part doesn't just change how others see you; it changes how you see yourself.

Owning your worth starts with belief in yourself and your ability to rise to the role you're stepping into. Sometimes, it's as simple as putting on a suit when everyone else is in jeans. And sometimes, it's about silencing that voice in your head that whispers, *Who do you think you are?*

THE VOICE OF DOUBT

If you're reading this, you've likely heard that voice before. Maybe it creeps in when you're about to raise your rates or introduce yourself as a health coach at a networking event. It whispers, *People will find out you don't really know what you're doing.* That voice has a name: impostor syndrome. It's especially common in the wellness industry, where comparison runs rampant.

I've seen countless health coaches hesitate to launch their practice, comparing their one-year certification to a doctor's twelve years of medical school. That comparison is not just unfair—it misses the point entirely. Health coaches aren't meant to do what doctors do. While doctors diagnose and treat medical conditions, health coaches help people make lasting lifestyle changes and navigate their daily wellness choices. You're not competing with doctors; you're complementing their work by providing the consistent support and guidance that most doctors simply don't have time to give. This isn't a lesser role; it's a vital one that fills a critical gap in healthcare.

But here's the thing about impostor syndrome: It keeps you stuck in preparation mode, always feeling like you need more credentials, more training, more everything before you can start. It's like standing at the edge of a cold pool, dipping your toe in, and convincing yourself it's too cold to swim. You hesitate, overthink, and make excuses. But when you finally jump in, minutes later, you wonder, *What took me so long?* Building your practice works the same way. You can spend months perfecting your Instagram page, fine-tuning your website, and tweaking your intake forms—or you can start helping people now. You just have to believe you are worth it.

When I founded IIN, I approached it with what some might call audacious confidence. Looking back, it might seem almost absurd—starting what would become the world's largest nutrition school without formal nutrition training myself. But I followed a simple guiding principle: As long as I knew more than the person I was counseling, I could help them. That's all it took.

Impostor syndrome thrives on the fear of being exposed as a fraud, but the truth is, you don't need to know everything to help someone. You just need to be one step ahead. The sooner you challenge those limiting beliefs, the sooner you can step into the role you were meant to play.

PROGRESS, NOT PERFECTION

One of the biggest misconceptions in the wellness industry is that you need to have perfect health to coach others. I've heard health coaches say, "I can't coach until I've overcome all my cravings" or "I'm not fit enough to inspire clients." But here's the truth: If you're doing your best to eat real food, move your body, and cultivate positivity in your life, you're already ahead of most people. That alone qualifies you to help others. Your imperfections don't disqualify you; they make you human.

Clients often prefer working with someone relatable, someone who has faced struggles similar to their own. Would you rather learn from someone who's navigated their own transformation or someone who's never had to overcome a challenge? Whether you're a coach, mentor, educator, entrepreneur, or leader, waiting until you've achieved some idealized state will only delay the impact you could be making right now. So don't worry if you're a few pounds over your ideal weight, still learning your craft, or refining your approach. The important thing is that you meet yourself where you are.

This isn't just about how you show up for others; it's also about how you show up for yourself. Truly owning your worth means recognizing that you are just as deserving of compassion and care as the people you support—imperfections and all. Those who are naturally compassionate toward others often forget to offer that same kindness to themselves. Make it a priority to extend the same care and understanding to yourself that you so freely give to your clients, students, or team members.

Self-compassion isn't optional; it's a necessity for sustainable success. When you make a mistake or face a setback, how do you speak to yourself? If your inner dialogue is harsh and unforgiving, you're making it harder to bounce back. Instead, try treating yourself with the same kindness you'd offer a good friend who was struggling. That emotional safety is what allows you to learn, grow, and try again.

BREAKING FREE FROM IMPOSTOR SYNDROME

So how do you break free from impostor syndrome and own your worth? Here are some strategies:

1. **Start Small**: I'm going to keep reiterating this one. Dive in, even if it's messy. Offer free sessions to friends or family. Share simple health tips online. Each small step builds confidence and momentum.

2. **Create a Confidence Support Network**: Surround yourself with like-minded entrepreneurs who understand your journey and can help you combat self-doubt. Join professional organizations, form a mastermind group, find mentors, or find an accountability partner focused on building confidence and celebrating your wins. Confidence grows when others help you challenge negative self-talk and recognize your true capabilities during moments of uncertainty.

3. **Create a Wins Folder**: Save every positive testimonial, thank-you note, and success story. When self-doubt creeps in, this folder becomes your antidote to impostor syndrome.

4. **Practice Micro-Confidence**: Tackle one small manageable task that feels slightly outside your comfort zone. Over time, these small wins compound into lasting confidence.

5. **Create New Evidence**: Challenge old beliefs through deliberate actions and affirmations. For example, if you believe you're not good enough to succeed at public speaking, start by setting incremental goals like sharing your thoughts in small meetings or community forums. Each time you speak up and receive positive feedback, you create new evidence that contradicts your limiting belief. The transformation won't happen overnight, but these small victories accumulate into a profound shift in your perspective over time.

EXERCISE: REFRAMING LIMITATIONS

Write down every reason you think you're not qualified enough to do this work. Got your list? Now, next to each item, write down how that very limitation might actually serve your clients. For example:

- "I'm not perfect with my own diet." → You understand the real-world challenges your clients face.
- "I'm new to the field." → You bring fresh perspective and current, up-to-date training.
- "I don't have decades of experience." → You remember what it's like to be at the beginning of a wellness journey.

THE CONFIDENCE DOMINO EFFECT

One of the most powerful realizations I've had in my career is that confidence isn't compartmentalized; it flows from one area of life into another. Think about something you excel at. Maybe you're a skilled soccer player, an amazing parent, or someone who can organize a chaotic space into perfect order. That confidence you feel in those areas? You can channel it into your career, even when you're just starting out. The self-assurance you feel on the soccer field or the competence you've developed as a parent can become the foundation for your professional growth.

Let me share a story about Elena, an IIN graduate. She came to me convinced she couldn't be a health coach because she was still working through her own weight loss journey. But Elena was an extraordinary elementary school teacher; she knew how to break down complex concepts, create supportive environments, and inspire growth in others. When she realized she could channel that teaching excellence into health coaching, everything shifted. Her weight was no longer a barrier; it became part of her story, making her more relatable to clients facing similar challenges.

This domino effect of confidence manifests in physical ways, too. I've noticed that when people invest in their physical strength—through workouts, yoga, or any form of movement that makes them feel powerful—that body confidence transfers into emotional confidence in everything they do. There's something transformative about feeling strong physically that empowers you to show up with more presence in meetings and speak with greater confidence in client sessions.

And, of course, confidence builds through action—each step you take creates momentum for the next. It's like learning to play tennis: You can't master it by reading a book. Sure, you can read about techniques, but you've got to get on the court to really learn the game. The same goes for working with clients. With your first client, you might feel like a deer in headlights. You might think, *Oh my god, what am I doing?* and feel like a fraud because you haven't been doing this for decades. But by your tenth client, you'll start finding your rhythm. Like tennis, when you get used to the back-and-forth across the net, you'll be in the game. Play another ten or twenty rounds, and suddenly, you'll find yourself moving with earned confidence and skill.

CRAFTING YOUR PROFESSIONAL PRESENCE

Remember my story about the suit? Let's dive deeper into what it means to look impeccable in your business. This isn't about following someone else's standards; it's about choosing how you present yourself to the world. When I started wearing suits to teach, something really interesting happened. Sure, I looked more professional, but that was just the beginning. Every time I put on that suit, it reminded me of the real value I was bringing to my students. It was like my own personal superhero costume. Looking sharp and put-together made me feel more confident, which made my students trust me more, which made me feel even more confident. It was like a domino effect of good energy. And while I'm using the suit as an example here, this same principle applies in so many ways—whether you're dressing up for in-person meetings or setting up your office in a way that's comfortable and inviting for your clients. It's all about finding what makes you feel like your best self so you can do your best work.

For you, looking impeccable might mean:

- Creating a clean, professional website that reflects your personality
- Developing organized, well-designed materials for your clients
- Maintaining a consistent, authentic social media presence
- Dressing in a way that makes you feel confident and competent

Just remember: While each element of your professional presence—from your website and your social media strategy to your client materials—matters, nothing should prevent you from getting started or serving clients. Avoid analysis paralysis—spending months tweaking your website colors or obsessing over your Instagram grid, using it as an excuse to avoid the real work of helping people. If you're choosing between having a perfect website and having your first client conversation, choose the conversation every time. You can always update your materials as you grow, but you can't get back the time you spend overthinking these details.

The goal is to be professional enough to make your clients feel confident in your services while not letting perfectionism keep you from actually providing those services. Start with clean, organized basics; then, focus your energy where it counts: becoming the best you can be for the people you serve.

BOUNDARIES AS SELF-RESPECT

The next step in owning your worth is setting boundaries to protect your time and energy. Boundaries aren't just about managing your schedule; they're an act of self-respect and a foundation for serving others effectively.

You can't say yes to everything, and you can't care deeply about everything. Knowing what matters most to you makes it easier to say no to things that drain your energy without contributing to your core mission. Setting boundaries doesn't make you selfish—it shows you're being strategic with your most precious resources: your time and energy.

Think about that friend who says yes to everything. They're constantly exhausted and overwhelmed but can't seem to turn down requests. Many new entrepreneurs fall into this trap—taking late-night calls, responding to client texts within minutes, and squeezing in just one more session on their day off. When you're passionate about helping others, saying no can feel uncomfortable or even wrong.

I once knew someone who struggled with boundaries so much that she began repeating this affirmation daily: "I have intrinsic value. I don't need to be constantly available or overgive to prove my worth." Let that sink in: Your worth isn't tied to how available you make yourself to others or how much you give. Embracing this truth can be transformative. In fact, maintaining healthy boundaries often helps you serve others with greater impact and clarity.

Boundaries are more than just a way to protect your time and energy; they're a statement of your value. Imagine a fence around a beautiful garden. Without it, anyone could trample the flowers or let their pets roam through your carefully tended beds. The fence isn't selfish; it's what allows the garden to flourish.

I learned this the hard way. Early in my career, while trying to keep the school afloat, I pushed myself far beyond my limits. I knew I was wrecking my health, but I kept going, convinced I had no other choice. While I trusted in my body's ability to heal, I realize now that setting proper boundaries would have been far wiser than planning to recover later.

Without boundaries, you send a message to the world that your time and energy are less valuable than everyone else's. This shows up in behaviors like accommodating clients who cancel last minute, taking on clients who can't afford your rates, or saying yes to things you don't want to do because you feel guilty saying no.

Every time you compromise your boundaries, you're not just

depleting yourself; you're teaching others how to treat you. And this pattern ripples into every part of your business, influencing everything from how much you charge to the kinds of clients you attract.

I've seen so many professionals cling to clients who drain their energy or constantly push boundaries simply because they're afraid to lose the income. But here's a perspective that might help: It's like dating. If you go on a date and the person is disrespectful or constantly demanding, would you agree to a second date? Maybe if you're desperate, you might. But a third date? Definitely not.

Yet in business, we often continue these unhealthy relationships simply because money is involved. I personally have no problem with ending these relationships. When I've had clients who weren't a good fit, I'd say, "You know, Joe, I hear what you're saying. This isn't working for you. Thank you for telling me this. I've decided I'm going to refund 100 percent of your money, and I'm sure you're going to find a better match. Have a nice day."

Just as you wouldn't compromise your standards in your personal life when you have options, you shouldn't compromise in your professional life either. If you had abundant cash flow, you'd likely make these decisions easily. The challenge is having the courage to uphold your boundaries even when you feel financially vulnerable.

The good news is that setting boundaries doesn't mean building walls. It's more like hosting a dinner party. You decide the time, the place, and the menu. You set expectations for when the meal starts and ends. Your guests don't show up at 3:00 a.m. demanding food, right? That's because you've set clear expectations. Professional boundaries work the same way: They create structure and clarity, allowing you to serve others on your terms.

Here's how to start creating boundaries that honor your worth:

1. **Create Clear Business Hours**: Set specific working hours and put them everywhere—your email signature, website, and client agreements. "Available Monday through Thursday, 9:00 a.m. to 5:00 p.m. EST" is a complete sentence. Make these hours sacred, just like a store's opening and closing times.

2. **Define Your Professional Scope**: Get crystal clear about what you do—and don't do. If you're a health coach, you're not a therapist or a doctor. It's okay (and necessary) to say, "That's outside my scope of practice. Let me refer you to someone who specializes in that."

3. **Protect Your Energy Blocks**: Block out time for self-care, family, and business development. These aren't extra or nice to have; they're essential for showing up as your best self for your clients. Think of these blocks as important as client meetings, because they are.

4. **Master the Graceful No**: Instead of elaborate excuses when you need to say no, try this: "Thank you for thinking of me. I need to decline, but I wish you all the best." Simple, kind, and clear. No justification needed.

What you'll realize is that clients actually respect you more when you set strong boundaries. Think about it: Would you trust a wellness coach who's clearly burned out and overwhelmed? Your boundaries signal that you value yourself and your work, which encourages clients to value you more in return. By setting and maintaining healthy boundaries, you're also modeling the self-respect and self-care that you want your clients to develop in their own lives.

The next time you feel that twinge of guilt about enforcing a boundary, remind yourself, *This is what owning my worth looks like in action. This is how I ensure I can serve others sustainably. This is how I build a business that honors both my gifts and my humanity.*

PRICING YOUR WORTH

Now that you've laid the groundwork for honoring your worth through boundaries, let's tackle another common challenge for new entrepreneurs: undercharging for your services. Many base their prices on what they think people can afford rather than the true value of what they offer. Let me be clear: If you can help someone transform their health—and, by extension, their life—that is priceless. Even if your service or product simply improves someone's daily life, that value is meaningful and deserves recognition.

When you undercharge, you're not just undervaluing yourself; you're undervaluing what you offer. Confident pricing reflects the worth of your work and signals to clients that you're serious about delivering results. Charging what you're worth doesn't just benefit you; it also attracts clients who are ready to commit and ensures that your business has the resources to grow and thrive.

That said, pricing isn't always straightforward. Sometimes, strategy takes precedence over confidence.

When IIN transitioned from live classes to online courses, my advisors recommended keeping our $8,950 price point. Instead, I took a calculated risk and cut the price in half. Many thought I was making a mistake, but I had a plan: If the program didn't succeed, I'd know it was the format, not the cost. It worked. Lowering the price increased accessibility, generated volume, and created a snowball effect as every two or three students referred another.

This example highlights an important nuance: Charging more isn't always the answer. Strategic pricing depends on your goals, market, and audience. With that in mind, here are three approaches to consider:

1. Help Community Leaders for Free

When starting out, offering your services for free to key community leaders can help you gain experience and build your reputation. Focus on people with influence, like church organizers or yoga instructors, who can spread the word about your work. While your time might theoretically be worth $200 an hour, if you're not working, that time has no monetary value. Strategic pro bono work can result in powerful testimonials and referrals that grow your network as you're building experience.

2. Use Tiered Pricing and Flexible Services

Create a range of pricing options—such as silver, gold, and platinum tiers—that cater to different budgets. Premium pricing can signal exclusivity and quality to some clients while group sessions or free resources can make your services accessible to a broader audience. Offering options ensures you can meet clients where they are without compromising your business goals.

3. Try the Freemium Model

For certain products or services, consider offering a free trial or free introductory content, followed by a modest fee (e.g., $12.95 per month). This approach allows potential clients to experience your value risk free, helping to build trust and encouraging them to invest further. Over time, this model can generate consistent income while expanding your reach.

Pricing your worth isn't simply about charging as much as you can; it's about aligning your strategy with your values and goals. Building a sustainable business allows you to fully commit to your mission and expand your reach so that your positive impact can continue and grow over time.

THE POWER OF PRESENCE

Next, let's talk about valuing your unique presence in your client interactions. For those whose work centers on helping others heal, grow, or transform, your presence isn't just part of the equation; it's often the most impactful part.

Here's a perspective-shifting truth for health coaches, wellness practitioners, and service-based entrepreneurs wrestling with impostor syndrome: You don't have to have all the answers to help others.

I often see people overcomplicate their practice with anxious thoughts, like *What do I say next?* or *Am I doing this right?* While it's helpful to have frameworks and techniques, supporting others isn't as complicated as many make it out to be. There's profound power in simply being present while someone speaks and resisting the urge to dominate the conversation.

When you show someone you're listening—*really* listening—something magical happens. Your client's brain recognizes the safety you've created, allowing them to access insights and solutions they couldn't access before. People have an incredible ability to find their own solutions when given the right space and support.

The mere act of listening catalyzes healing and release. Watch what happens when a child falls down: They cry out, "Ahhhhh!"—and moments later, they're fine. That release is actually necessary for becoming whole again. Adults aren't so different. Mostly, we all just want to be heard. When we're upset or stressed, we rarely need advice; advice is everywhere. What we need is someone fully present who can hold space for us and listen—especially in today's distracted world.

Think about it: How often have you helped someone just by listening? That's not a coincidence. It's an innate human ability encoded in our DNA. As a coach, your presence and empathy are often more valuable than any advice you might offer. You don't need to master a complicated system to support your clients. Formal techniques and frameworks are just tools to enhance what's already naturally within you.

As you develop trust in the power of your presence, you'll begin to recognize that your impact extends far beyond individual client sessions. What may seem like small moments of holding space and deep listening can create ripples that transform not just individuals but entire communities. This brings us to an even bigger truth about your potential impact in the world.

ONE PERSON'S POTENTIAL IMPACT

Throughout my life, I've been fascinated by how a single individual can create enormous change. This idea took root when I was young and heard visionary architect Buckminster Fuller speak about the transformative power of one person acting with intention. His message—that a single individual, through deliberate action, could reshape the world—captivated me.

I've seen this principle play out firsthand—not because I'm special or uniquely talented, but because I approached my goals with what I call single-pointed focus: the practice of directing all of my attention and energy toward one clear objective. When you eliminate distractions and commit fully to your vision, remarkable things become possible.

This principle becomes especially powerful when you're questioning your worth or doubting your impact. You might look at industry leaders and think they have something special that you don't. But every person who's made a difference started exactly where you are now. The only difference is a willingness to take committed action, express your authentic self, and create positive change.

The health and wellness field is particularly rife with this kind of individual impact. While many practitioners focus solely on personal health journeys, I urge you to think bigger—to consider how your work addresses our broader healthcare crisis. The possibilities for health coaches and wellness professionals are boundless in a world where hundreds of millions of people still don't understand how processed foods affect their health and their children's future. Your knowledge and guidance can help transform this reality, one person, one family, one community at a time.

The bottom line is that you're capable of more than you think—and the ripples of change you create can reach farther than you imagine. So try not to let fear hold you back. By staying grounded in your mission to make a difference, you'll naturally attract opportunities and success. Your ability to improve lives is a powerful gift, and when you embrace it fully, you'll see just how far your impact can go.

Take a moment to reflect on your own impact journey:

- Think about a time when your actions created positive change in someone's life.
- Recall moments when you felt most proud of your accomplishments.
- Consider instances where you overcame self-doubt to achieve something meaningful.

These memories aren't just feel-good moments; they're evidence of your power to create change. Return to these experiences whenever doubt creeps in. They're your personal proof that one person—*you*—can indeed make a profound difference.

———

When you step fully into your worth, you empower others to do the same. Every time you price your services to reflect your value, show up professionally despite your fears, or share your knowledge despite that voice of doubt, you're not just building your business; you're contributing to a larger positive shift in the world.

I've watched health coaching grow from a tiny niche to a multibillion-dollar industry. This growth didn't happen because people waited until they felt completely ready. It happened because people like you decided to begin, trust their training, and believe in the unique value they could provide.

Your journey to owning your worth extends beyond business success; it creates space for your highest contribution to the world. When you truly own your worth, you give yourself permission to serve at your highest level. That's what this work is really about.

REFLECTION QUESTIONS

1. What simple actions can you take to project confidence and professionalism in your work?

2. How has self-doubt or impostor syndrome shown up for you, and how can you challenge it?

3. In what ways could your imperfections make you more relatable and effective as a guide for others?

4. What boundaries could you set to better honor your time, energy, and worth?

5. How can your unique skills or knowledge create positive change in your community or beyond?

8

—

REACH
YOUR PEOPLE

Marketing and *networking*—just hearing those words might make you want to disappear. As a heart-driven entrepreneur, the idea of promoting yourself may bring up tension in your body. That knot in your stomach when you consider selling your services isn't uncommon. In fact, I hear people say all the time:

- "It feels wrong to promote myself."
- "I don't want to seem pushy."
- "I'm here to help people, not sell things."

Let's sit with that discomfort for a moment. Where does it come from? Often, it stems from a genuine place of wanting to serve others, not profit from their struggles. Maybe you've had experiences with aggressive salespeople who made you feel pressured or manipulated.

Or perhaps you've seen wellness professionals who seemed more focused on their bottom line than their clients' well-being. When marketing is associated with tactics like persuasion and pressure, it can feel misaligned with your values.

But authentic marketing is something entirely different. It's not about convincing people to buy; it's about connection. It's about showing up as your true self, clearly expressing what you offer, and trusting that the right people will recognize you as the person they've been searching for. When done with integrity, marketing isn't pushy; it's an act of service. By being visible in a way that aligns with your values, you create a bridge between your work and those who truly need it.

Think about it this way: If you have the ability to help someone ease chronic pain, find peace in their body, or transform their relationship with stress, isn't it actually a disservice to keep that hidden? Every time you stay quiet about your work, someone who needs your support might remain stuck in their suffering. The people who need you are out there searching—not for just any solution, but for the right one. Your job is to show them that you're the answer they've been seeking.

I learned something powerful about this when designing the IIN logo. When we created the red spiral, everyone had an opinion. "Red is too aggressive." "Red represents violence." But my gut told me otherwise, and I knew that playing it safe wasn't the point. Red is the color of blood, and food becomes our blood, which becomes our thoughts and feelings. Red represents the passion of our students and the energy of life itself. And the spiral? Spirals appear everywhere in nature—in our fingerprints, in seashells, even in the way galaxies move through space. They represent connection, growth, and the ripple effect created by the IIN community.

The red spiral wasn't just a logo; it was like sending out a signal that would resonate with exactly the right people. Those who were meant to find us would be drawn to its energy, its boldness, its natural symbolism. Some people didn't get it, and that was exactly the point: They weren't our people. When you market yourself authentically, it works the same way: Your message becomes a beacon that naturally attracts those who need exactly what you offer.

Authentic marketing is not about being pushy or salesy or using clever tactics to get people to buy things. And it's not about appealing to everyone. It's about building trust, transparency, and genuine relationships—focusing on connecting with those who truly resonate with what you offer.

SERVE; DON'T SELL

Here's my golden rule: "I'm never selling; I'm always serving." That mindset shift changes everything.

When I launched Knew Health, I didn't start by thinking about how to sell medical cost-sharing memberships. Instead, I asked myself, *What problem am I solving?* The answer was simple: People hate their insurance companies. By focusing on that pain point and offering a solution, I wasn't selling; I was helping.

The same is true no matter what kind of work you do. Whether you're a coach, a therapist, a wellness practitioner, or a creative, the people you serve are already looking for solutions. Your job is to be the person who truly sees them, understands their struggles, and shows up with confidence to offer a clear path forward.

Think about a time when someone asked what you do and you hesitated, downplayed it, or brushed it off. Maybe you felt awkward or didn't want to sound self-promotional. But imagine if, instead of shrinking back, you simply shared what you do in a way that highlights why it matters. If you're an acupuncturist, for example, and someone casually mentions their constant migraines, you don't have to sell them on booking a session. You can just share, "That's actually something I help people with all the time. Acupuncture can be really effective for migraines." No pressure, no pitch—just a simple, genuine way of letting them know you can help.

People respond to sincerity. When you show up with genuine enthusiasm for what you do and a clear understanding of how it helps, the right people will recognize it, and the connection will happen naturally.

CASE STUDY: MARCUS THE WEB DEVELOPER

When Marcus left his corporate tech job to start his freelance web development business, he quickly realized that traditional marketing wasn't for him. Cold emails felt impersonal, networking events were draining, and competing on price was a race to the bottom.

So, instead of trying to sell his services, Marcus focused on helping. He started paying close attention to online forums and local business groups in which small business owners vented about website issues. Whenever he saw a question he could answer, he jumped in—not with a sales pitch, but with clear, useful advice.

One day, a restaurant owner posted in a local Facebook group, frustrated that her online menu wouldn't load on mobile phones. Marcus responded with a quick explanation of the issue and a simple fix the owner could try herself. A few days later, the restaurant owner messaged him: "Tried your suggestion—worked like a charm! We actually need a full site update. Can you help?"

Moments like that started happening more often. Business owners appreciated that Marcus wasn't pushing his services; he was just helping. And when they needed more than a quick fix, he was the first person they thought of.

Within a year, Marcus had built a steady stream of clients without running ads, making sales calls, or offering discounts. He didn't have to chase leads; they came to him, because he had already proven his value.

"The biggest lesson I learned," Marcus says, "is that people don't want to be sold to. They want to feel like someone actually cares about their problem. When you focus on serving instead of selling, trust builds naturally—and the business follows."

AUTHENTIC NETWORKING
FOR SENSITIVE SOULS

I'll be real with you: I'm terrible at traditional networking. As an HSP, the idea of mingling in a crowded room feels like a nightmare. I avoid most networking events and rarely put myself in situations to meet new people. So when someone asks if I know this person or that person, I usually just say, "Nope," because I honestly don't know many people.

I see others working a room like it's nothing: They chat easily, listen, and bounce from person to person without a second thought. But for me, it's completely different. I'm hyperaware of everything: how I'm standing, what people are saying (or not saying), their tone of voice, what they're wearing, and even subtle shifts in the energy of the room. While everyone else is just having normal conversations, I feel like my brain is burning through 200 units of energy a minute. It's exhausting.

Maybe you can relate. I'm happiest when I'm like Superman in his Fortress of Solitude. That's where I thrive—alone in my quiet space, doing what I do best.

But here's the thing: Even though I avoid traditional networking like the plague, I somehow keep meeting the right people at the right time. It's as if the universe sends them my way when it's meant to happen. Connections happen naturally, without me forcing anything. It's not that I'm actively trying to network; I'm just doing my thing, staying true to what I'm passionate about, and somehow the right opportunities and connections come effortlessly.

This has led me to develop some gentle approaches to connecting with others—ways that don't drain my energy or feel fake. If you're a fellow sensitive soul looking to grow your network without the overwhelm, here are some strategies that have worked for me.

SIMPLE WAYS TO REACH YOUR PEOPLE

1. START WITH YOUR EXISTING NETWORK

Before you cast your net wide, start with the network you already have: friends, family, former colleagues, and even casual acquaintances. These are the people who already know, like, and trust you, making them the perfect place to begin.

Reach out with a thoughtful email, a personal phone call, or a conversation over coffee. Let them know what you're working on and how they can support you—whether that's spreading the word, offering feedback, or even becoming a client themselves. This isn't pushing or selling; it's inviting them into a conversation.

Your existing network can also be a powerful referral source. When people see your passion and genuine desire to help, they're more likely to connect you with someone who could benefit from your work. Sometimes, the opportunities you're looking for are just one degree away from the people you already know.

Additionally, consider the resources you already have at your disposal. Maybe you have a strong social media following, an email list you haven't engaged with in a while, or connections through community groups or online forums. Reach out and start conversations. Share what you have to offer, and let your network know how they can help.

The key here is authenticity. Approach your network with

openness and sincerity, not as a sales pitch. People who know you are often the most willing to help; they just need to know how.

EXERCISE: FIVE PEOPLE IN YOUR NETWORK

Take five minutes right now to write down five people you already know who might benefit from your work or could introduce you to someone who would.

When you're ready to reach out, here's a customizable email template you can use as a guide:

> Hi, [Name],
>
> I hope you're doing well! It's been a while since we've connected, and I wanted to reach out to share something exciting that I've been working on.
>
> I'm currently [describe your project, business, or initiative—what it's about and who it's for]. I'm so passionate about helping [your ideal client—who you help and why], and I wanted to let you know in case you or someone you know might benefit from what I'm offering.
>
> If you'd be open to it, I'd truly appreciate your support in any of these ways:
>
> **Spread the word on social:** If you feel moved by my work, sharing it on your social channels could help it reach others who might need it. Even a simple post or story can make a big difference.

Feedback or ideas: I'd be grateful for any feedback you might have or suggestions on places where I could share my work.

Connect me: If you know anyone who might be interested, a personal recommendation or introduction would mean the world to me.

Of course, there's no expectation; I'm simply grateful for your time. I'd love to reconnect soon regardless, even if it's just for a quick chat or coffee to catch up.

Thank you so much for taking the time to read this, and I hope to hear from you soon!

Warmly,
[Your Name]

2. POSITION YOURSELF AS A GUIDE

When you share your message—whether it's on your website, in newsletters, or on social media—remember that people aren't just looking for information. They can find that anywhere. They're looking for someone who truly gets them—someone who deeply understands their struggles and can show them the way forward.

Share stories that show you've walked this path before. Write about the problems you see people facing in a way that makes them feel truly seen. Then, show them there's hope, that you understand not just their surface challenges but the deeper impact these challenges have on their lives.

Being a guide doesn't mean acting like an expert who talks down to people; it means combining genuine empathy with real solutions. When you do connect with potential clients, they'll already sense that you understand their journey and have the competence to help them move forward.

Let me show you what I mean. Here are two wellness practitioners writing about stress management:

- *First Approach:* "As a certified stress management expert with three degrees, I can tell you that 63 percent of Americans are managing stress incorrectly. My proven five-step scientific method will fix that for you."

- *Second Approach:* "I remember lying awake at 3:00 a.m., my mind racing with deadlines and responsibilities. Like you, I tried everything: meditation apps, breathing exercises, even counting sheep. What I discovered through my own journey and through walking alongside dozens of others is that managing stress isn't about following a perfect protocol. It's about finding your own rhythm. I'd love to show you how to discover yours."

Can you feel the difference? The first approach feels distant and leaves the reader feeling judged. The second meets them where they are, offering understanding and guidance while showing competence through experience rather than credentials. Be the guide who connects, inspires trust, and makes people feel truly seen.

3. GIVE BEFORE YOU ASK

Think of your business like dating: You wouldn't propose on the first date, right? Instead, you'd spend time getting to know each other, building trust, and creating a connection over time. Business works the same way. Start by sharing your knowledge generously, and let people experience the value you offer.

One of the best marketing lessons I ever learned came from the early days of IIN. When I started the school, I was just a guy who had moved to New York from Canada, trying to get the word out. I didn't have a big advertising budget, so I created a magazine called *Gulliver's* (later renamed to *Integrative Nutrition*). It was filled with great holistic health content, modeled after the free newspapers you'd pick up on the street, like *The Village Voice* or *The Free Press*. I printed a limited number of issues and distributed them in natural food stores and restaurants, knowing they would land in the right hands.

That magazine was my only marketing. People would pick it up, flip through it, and think, *What is this? I've never seen anything like it.* Then, by the end, they'd realize it was connected to a school. And that was how they found out about IIN. I knew the right people would resonate with it. Meanwhile, I wasn't hustling all year; I'd go to India in the summer, come back in August or September, put out the magazine, and by late October, people were signing up for classes.

But my generosity didn't stop there. When people came to the school, I'd have a buffet of incredible food waiting for them. Between the magazine and the food, I was giving, giving, giving. And without realizing it, people were moving down the funnel, thinking, *I can't say no to this guy; he's got everything.*

You might worry about giving too much away for free or feel the need to hold something back, but the truth is, the more you give, the more people will trust that you have even more to offer. Be generous with your knowledge and expertise—create newsletters that teach something valuable, share genuinely helpful content on social media, offer free webinars or downloads, and share case studies that highlight real transformation. The more value you consistently deliver, the more naturally people come to see you as an expert in your field. It's like advertising without advertising—rather than telling people you're an authority, you're showing them through your knowledge and the value you provide. Just like a great appetizer before a meal, your free content gives people a taste of what they can expect, creating a natural demand for what you do.

Just keep in mind that while giving is key, setting boundaries is equally important. Offering free content helps build trust, but don't feel obligated to provide unlimited one-on-one advice. Set clear guidelines for how you work, protect your time, and avoid over-giving in ways that don't align with your business goals. Be sure to communicate how you operate and what's available, ensuring that your generosity supports both your clients and your well-being.

4. MEET THEM WHERE THEY ARE

This concept has a double meaning. First, it's about reaching potential clients in the places they already spend time. Second, it's about connecting with them emotionally—understanding their current struggles, needs, and goals and meeting them with empathy right where they are in their journey.

Years ago, when I created my magazine, I left it in natural food stores and restaurants where my ideal audience would naturally come across it. Obviously, a lot has changed in the past thirty years—today's world is much more online—but the principle remains the same. You need to identify where your potential clients already spend their time, whether that's a local yoga studio, a specific Facebook group, or an industry conference.

EXERCISE: PLACES THEY GATHER

Make a list of places—both online and offline—where your potential clients gather. This could be

- Facebook groups
- LinkedIn discussions
- Online forums
- In-person meetups
- Community centers, studios, or co-working spaces
- Industry conferences

Next, you're going to want to join the conversation and position yourself as someone who can be of service. But first, listen. Your ability to empathize and connect is your greatest strength in marketing. What are people struggling with? What kinds of conversations are happening? Where can you add insight? Start by observing; then, slowly start contributing to discussions by offering thoughtful comments, sharing helpful resources, or asking questions that deepen discussions. Think of it as engaging in meaningful conversations rather than trying to win business. Instead of pitching your services, focus on building trust. When people see you as a valuable, engaged presence in their space, they'll naturally become curious about what you have to offer.

For example, if you're a wellness coach and you see a discussion about stress management, don't jump in with a sales pitch. Instead, you might say:

> "I totally get how overwhelming stress can be. One approach I've found really effective is a 'sensory reset ritual'—a quick practice that uses specific sounds, scents, and grounding techniques to interrupt the stress cycle. It's simple but surprisingly powerful—happy to share more if that's helpful!"

This keeps the conversation organic, warm, and non-salesy—and over time, these small interactions lead to deeper relationships and potential clients.

5. CHOOSE YOUR CHANNELS WISELY

Marketing doesn't have to drain you. If writing energizes you but video feels like a chore, focus on writing. If large events exhaust you but small gatherings light you up, stick to intimate workshops or one-on-one interactions. There's no one-size-fits-all in authentic marketing. You're allowed to choose the channels where you can show up comfortably and connect in ways that feel true to you. And don't feel pressure to do everything. It's better to do a few things really well than spread yourself too thin trying to keep up with every trend. Stay true to what feels authentic, and your audience will feel it, too.

6. CREATE A MOVEMENT, NOT JUST A MESSAGE

Your work isn't just about selling a product or service; it's about creating something people want to be part of. Share stories that inspire, start conversations that matter, and cultivate a sense of community.

Think of the famous line from *Field of Dreams*: "If you build it, they will come." In the film, this phrase represents a leap of faith—the idea that if you create something meaningful and worthwhile, the right people will show up. The same applies to your business. When you focus on creating value and authentic connections, people naturally gravitate toward you. They'll want to be part of what you're building—not because you're pushing it on them, but because they feel like they belong.

This approach isn't just good for business; it's fulfilling on a deeper level. It reconnects you with your purpose: to help, to connect, and to make a difference. Marketing that aligns with who you are isn't just effective; it feels right.

BE FULLY THERE

If you're a health coach, life coach, therapist, or anyone who works with clients one-on-one, there's another vital aspect of reaching and serving your people: the quality of your presence. It's not just about what you say or do; it's about how fully you show up. This might seem separate from marketing, but in reality, it's one of the most important parts. Being fully present builds trust, deepens connections, and helps your business grow through word of mouth.

People have a natural sense of whether they're being heard. If you're at a party and someone asks what you do for a living, you naturally adjust your response based on whether they seem gen-uinely interested or just making conversation. The same thing happens with clients. They unconsciously gauge how much to share based on how present and engaged you are.

If your mind is elsewhere—on your to-do list, dinner plans, or what you'll say next—your clients will notice. They might hold back, stay on the surface, and have fewer breakthroughs. Similarly, if you're overbooked, overwhelmed, or running on empty, they'll pick up on that, too. Energy isn't invisible; they can sense when you're depleted or distracted. That's why prioritizing your own well-being is essen-tial. The more you care for your energy, the more fully you can show up for your clients. And when they feel deeply seen and supported, they're more likely to return and recommend you to others.

QUICK GROUNDING EXERCISE: THE 3-2-1 RESET

Before client sessions, meetings, or other high-stakes conver-sations, take a minute to center yourself so you can be fully present. Try this simple practice:

- **3 Breaths:** Take three deep, slow breaths, allowing each exhale to relax your body. Let go of mental noise, and shift your awareness from your thoughts into your heart and body.

- **2 Senses:** Notice two things you can hear and two things you can feel—maybe your breath, the hum of a fan, the weight of your body in your chair. If scents help

> you stay grounded, keep an essential oil on hand, and
> take a deep inhale to anchor yourself in the present.
> - **1 Intention:** Set a simple intention, like "I am here to
>   listen fully" or "My presence is my gift."

As you step into your session or conversation, stay rooted in the present. If your mind drifts to the past or future, gently bring it back. Make eye contact. Listen not just with your ears but with your whole being.

Being fully present deepens trust and connection, which is the foundation of any successful business. When you show up authentically and attentively, clients feel valued and understood, leading to lasting relationships, repeat business, and referrals. Prioritizing presence is an investment in both your clients' success and your own.

THE COURAGE TO BE SEEN

With everything we've covered in this chapter, you might still feel a little vulnerable about putting yourself out there—and that's completely natural. Sharing your work with the world means allowing yourself to be seen. And being seen—truly seen—can feel scary, especially when you care deeply about the work you do.

Whether you're launching a program, sharing your art, opening a private practice, or promoting your business, you're not just offering a service; you're sharing a part of yourself—your values, your perspective, your voice. It takes courage to say, "This is what I believe in," and "This is how I can help."

I see so many people in our field trying to come across as these perfect, polished experts—like they've got it all figured out and have never stumbled along the way. But here's the thing: That's like trying to teach someone to ride a bike while pretending you've never fallen off one yourself. It's the moments when we share our own journey—including the doubts we've worked through and the lessons we've learned—that we create the deepest connections with others.

Now, this doesn't mean you need to share every detail of your personal life or turn your marketing into a therapy session. But it does mean letting enough of your real self shine through so that the right people can think, *Yes, this person gets it. They understand where I'm coming from.* The very qualities that make you nervous about being visible—maybe you're naturally quiet, or highly sensitive, or tend to process things deeply—might be exactly what your ideal clients are looking for.

———

In the end, marketing isn't about pushing or performing; it's about showing up fully, sharing authentically, and trusting that your work will resonate with those who need it most. The strategies we've talked about aren't tricks or techniques; they're ways of putting your work into the world that feel true to you.

When you focus on serving instead of selling, when you stay true to your natural way of connecting, and when you find the courage to be visible, real relationships start to grow. Success doesn't come from marketing perfectly; it comes from marketing authentically.

REFLECTION QUESTIONS

1. What emotions or beliefs come up for you when you think about marketing your work?

2. How could reframing marketing as a beacon for those who need you shift your approach?

3. Think about your existing network. Who are three people you could reach out to this week?

4. Which marketing channels naturally energize you, and which ones drain you?

5. How present are you really being in your client interactions, and what might change if you deepened your presence?

9

DON'T FREAK OUT

Ten years ago, I was traveling in Asia to visit a new longevity clinic created by graduates of my school. After a routine blood test, I heard the words nobody ever wants to hear: "You have cancer!" I was diagnosed with chronic lymphocytic leukemia (CLL), a genetic cancer that had already claimed the lives of other family members. The version I had was aggressive and incurable. Neither radiation nor chemotherapy would stop the inevitable progress of this disease.

My initial reaction was shock. Then, I made jokes, prompting the doctor to look at me with bewilderment. He could not understand why I was laughing in the face of cancer. He had given this diagnosis to hundreds of patients, and no one reacted quite like this. But beneath the humor, I felt an unshakable trust that I would be okay.

My white blood cell count was rising fast. But even as the numbers climbed—first to 12, then 14, eventually to 150—I understood that panicking wouldn't make anything better. I had to become a calm, analytical problem-solver.

I refused to accept that my condition was beyond help. I sought out alternative treatments in Germany, Mexico, and Florida. Some treatments felt like scams targeting desperate cancer patients while others offered glimmers of hope. I spent a lot of time and money, but I never stopped looking for answers. When one path didn't work, I pivoted and kept moving forward.

During one treatment, I connected with a nurse who was caring for me daily, and we started getting to know each other. One day, she told me about her daughter—how she'd gotten into a prestigious science program but couldn't afford it. Without hesitation, I offered to help. "I'll give you the money," I said. The nurse broke down in tears and gave me a huge hug I'll never forget.

A few weeks later, she leaned in and shared something shocking. "I just have to tell you, Mr. Rosenthal," she whispered, "the reason your blood count is going down isn't the expensive experimental drug the doctor is giving you. It's because of the low-dose thalidomide you're taking." She explained the doctor was trying to experiment, hoping to patent some breakthrough treatment. In other words, the doctor had been using me as a test subject while charging me a small fortune, when a simple, low-cost medication was actually making my blood count improve.

Immediately, I left that doctor and tried a new FDA-approved medication. It worked, but the side effects—fatigue, joint pain, and depression—were brutal. Exhausted and frustrated, I sought better options. That's when I discovered the CLL Society, a nonprofit organization started by Dr. Brian Koffman. Through their network, I connected with specialists who introduced me to better treatment options—and experimental prescriptions that worked without the side effects.

In case you're wondering how this relates to business, looking back, I realize that if I hadn't been calm and persistent, I wouldn't be here today. Like a Roomba hitting a wall, I didn't panic; I recalibrated and kept moving. That mindset saved my life and reinforced what I've always believed: Don't settle for the first answer you're given. Ask questions, stay alert, and trust your intuition—whether in health, business, or life. If one door closes, another door will open—but only if you keep searching with a clear head. Panicking will only cloud your judgment and keep you stuck. The right answers are out there, but they require resilience, resourcefulness, and focus.

Staying calm and adaptable wasn't just how I survived cancer; it's how I've navigated my entire career. When things go wrong, the best response is to stay centered, assess your options, and move forward. Put simply: Don't freak out.

So how can you put this into action when the pressure's on?

RELEASING EGO AND FEAR

Staying calm in business starts with knowing when to step back from your ego. There's a concept from Eastern philosophy called die before you die. It may sound dramatic, but it's actually pretty practical. It's about letting go of ego-driven fears, attachments, and the urge to control everything. Doing so creates space for greater clarity, focus, and emotional resilience.

In business—especially if you're operating a service-based practice—this mindset can be transformative. Picture a client canceling sessions, leaving a gap in your income. Or maybe a workshop you poured your heart into attracts fewer people than expected. These situations can trigger feelings of frustration, self-doubt, or panic. When those emotions take over, it's easy to fall into fear-based reactions: offering discounts, taking on clients who aren't a good fit, or overworking to compensate for lost income.

On the other hand, you could observe your initial response, then ask, *What would I do if I weren't afraid of this outcome?* and *How can I respond thoughtfully instead of reacting impulsively?* This shift helps you meet challenges with curiosity and creativity. A client who cancels becomes an opportunity to reach out to new prospects. A disappointing workshop turnout might prompt you to experiment with your marketing or adjust your offerings to better meet your audience's needs. Releasing attachment to specific outcomes keeps you grounded in your broader vision.

My drive to approach life and business this way stems from my childhood. Growing up as the child of concentration camp survivors, I was acutely aware of life's fragility. This shaped my priorities. I cared deeply about making the world a better place because of the unspeakable horrors my parents endured. My purpose became creating impact, even in the face of setbacks.

In business, this perspective is powerful. Accepting that life—and business—is unpredictable frees you from chasing perfection. Instead, you focus on what truly matters: impact, growth, and integrity. Setbacks aren't the end of the story; they're part of the process. Releasing fear and ego helps you take risks, recover from failures, and stay true to your values, even when things don't go as planned.

To connect with this idea of die before you die, try the following exercise. It might be tough, but what it reveals can be profoundly valuable.

EXERCISE: YOUR LEGACY VISION

Imagine your own funeral. Picture the people who matter most to you gathering to celebrate your life.

- What qualities or contributions would you want to be remembered for?
- What values would you hope to have embodied?
- How will the world be different because you lived?

Now, apply this to your business.

- What deeper purpose do you want your work to serve?
- How can you contribute to your field in a way that reflects your values?
- What lasting impact do you hope to leave on your clients, community, or industry?

I first encountered this exercise during a workshop in India. Part of the practice involved meditating on your life as though it had already passed. Reflecting on mortality can quickly reconnect you with your deeper values and clarify the kind of impact you want your work to have.

Releasing ego and fear allows you to see your business clearly. It creates space to pause, gain perspective, and respond to challenges thoughtfully. This mindset forms the foundation of situational awareness—the ability to stay grounded, notice what's really happening, and make intentional decisions.

SITUATIONAL AWARENESS

When the doctor told me about my cancer diagnosis, it felt like part of me stepped back and watched the whole scene unfold from a distance. I could see myself, the doctor, the room we were in—even feel the emotions swirling around—but I wasn't overwhelmed by them. I was calm, focused, and clear, as if viewing everything through a wide lens.

This ability to step back and observe is what I call situational awareness. It's a term borrowed from the military, where it refers to having a 360-degree view of your environment and understanding how all the moving parts fit together. In business and leadership, it's about staying calm and clearheaded so you can make better decisions instead of just reacting impulsively.

I've felt this in other situations as well. For example, during arguments with my ex-wife, instead of reacting in the heat of the moment, I'd pause and wonder, *What's really going on here? Am I really a terrible person? Or could it be that she's tired? Hungry? Frustrated?* I'd listen to her words while also paying attention to her tone, body language, and emotions. This broader awareness helped me step back and understand the bigger picture of what was happening instead of being consumed by the immediate tension.

When a challenge comes up in business—like having a tense conversation with a stressed-out client—it's easy to get caught up in the immediate issue. But situational awareness helps you take a step back. What else might be affecting the situation? How is the client really feeling? Are there outside pressures influencing their response? By keeping an eye on the bigger picture, you can make smarter, more thoughtful decisions instead of letting your emotions take over.

Situational awareness is different from dissociation. Dissociation disconnects you from reality due to stress or trauma, leaving you numb or checked out. Situational awareness, on the other hand, grounds you in the present while expanding your perspective. It allows you to see beyond the immediate issue and think through all the contributing factors.

This skill has helped me in countless areas, including speaking in front of audiences. When I'm on stage, I make it a point to get out of my head and into my body. I focus on grounding myself, feeling my feet on the floor, and taking in the energy of the room. I read the audience—not just their words or reactions but their posture, energy, and engagement. This presence allows me to connect more deeply, tailoring my message to what they need in the moment.

Situational awareness has also sharpened my listening skills when I counsel people. I notice patterns quickly—just by observing someone, I can often get a sense of their personality and what they might need. For example, I might think, *This person seems like an extrovert who feels things deeply.* It's not about putting people into boxes but about understanding them better so I can support them more effectively.

In high-stress situations, situational awareness becomes vital. During all the challenging times at IIN and Knew Health, I learned to resist giving in to emotional desperation. Instead, I'd take a deep breath, drink a glass of water, and remind myself, *It's all meant to be. What's the best thing I can do right now?* That calm space created the clarity I needed to make the next right move.

While emotions offer valuable insights, they aren't the full picture. They shift constantly, and sometimes, they can lead us in the wrong direction. By stepping back and considering the bigger picture, we can make more informed decisions. It's like seeing the forest instead of just the trees.

THE POWER OF MENTAL REHEARSAL

Staying calm and maintaining situational awareness isn't just about what you do in the moment; it's also about how you prepare yourself mentally. One of the most powerful tools I've found is something athletes call visualization, but I like to think of it as mental rehearsal. It's like watching a movie in your mind of how you want things to go.

This isn't just positive thinking or daydreaming; it's actually rewiring your brain for success. When you take time to visualize something in detail, your brain builds new pathways, almost like it's practicing the real thing. That's why Olympic athletes dedicate so much time to mental rehearsal. They visualize every aspect of their performance, including things that might go wrong, so when the moment arrives, their mind and body already know exactly what to do.[8]

You can use this same technique in business and life. Before any situation that matters to you—whether it's a presentation, a difficult conversation, or unveiling a new offering—take a few quiet moments to play it through in your mind. See yourself staying composed, even if things don't go as planned. Feel what it's like to respond thoughtfully instead of reacting. Picture yourself navigating challenges with grace. Try it; you'll be amazed.

---

8   ROADSTARZ Sports Education Ltd, "The Power of Visualisation in Sports and Business—Seeing Is Believing," May 26, 2023, https://www.linkedin.com/pulse/power-visualisation-sports-business-seeing-believeing.

But here's the part most people miss: Effective visualization isn't just about seeing everything go perfectly. It's about mentally preparing for different possibilities, including the challenging ones. When you've already "experienced" various scenarios in your mind, you're better equipped to handle whatever actually happens without freaking out.

For example, if you're preparing for an important client presentation, don't just visualize everyone nodding along and loving your ideas. Take time to imagine what you'll do if someone raises tough questions or seems skeptical. See yourself staying calm, taking a deep breath, and responding thoughtfully rather than defensively. Picture yourself saying something like, "That's actually a great point; let me address that," and then walking through your response. When you've mentally rehearsed staying composed during challenging moments, you're much less likely to be thrown off balance when they actually happen. It's like having a dress rehearsal for your composure.

The beauty of this practice is that it's available to you anytime, anywhere. You don't need special equipment or training—just a few minutes of quiet time to mentally rehearse. And the more you practice, the more natural it becomes to stay centered and clearheaded when pressure hits.

"DON'T FIRE UNTIL YOU SEE THE WHITES OF THEIR EYES"

Once you've learned to step back and see the bigger picture, and prepare for different scenarios through visualization, the next challenge is timing—knowing when to act and when to wait, because timing is everything.

There's an old military saying I live by: "Don't fire until you see the whites of their eyes." It comes from the Battle of Bunker Hill, where Colonel William Prescott told his soldiers to wait until the enemy was close enough to make every shot count. In business and life, this means finding the right moment to act—not too early, not too late.

This is especially tricky if you're a people pleaser or a perfectionist. You might fall into one of two camps: Either you jump in too quickly, trying to fix things before fully understanding the situation, or you get stuck overthinking everything until good opportunities pass you by. Both reactions stem from the same place: fear. They just look different on the outside.

I put this principle to the test during one of the most challenging periods at IIN. For three years, the New York State Board of Education threatened to shut us down, claiming we didn't comply with their rules. At the same time, we faced persistent pressure from the American Dietetic Association and the American Psychological Association. When they finally summoned me to a hearing in Albany and announced they were closing the school, I had a tough choice to make. We had students who'd already paid tuition that we couldn't refund. I couldn't hide the problem, but I also couldn't let panic take over.

Instead of reacting impulsively, I chose to trust that the right opportunity would present itself. At one of our events, I remained composed on stage, modeling calm confidence for our students. I casually mentioned that we were dealing with some regulatory challenges and asked if anyone might have connections with elected officials in New York state.

Right then, a woman in the audience came down from the balcony and said, "My father can help you. He knows everybody." That one connection changed everything. He had connections with all the right people, and somehow—magically, mysteriously—the problem evaporated. Truly a miracle!

The key was sharing the problem at the right time and in the right way. Too early, and I would have caused unnecessary panic. Too late, and we might have missed the help we desperately needed. Because I didn't react out of fear, I created space for a solution to emerge.

This kind of patience is difficult—especially if you're someone who feels a strong sense of responsibility for others. The trick is practicing what I call active waiting—staying alert and ready while allowing things to develop. Think of it like surfing. A good surfer doesn't paddle at the first wave they see or sit there forever waiting for the perfect one. They watch, learn the patterns, and choose their moment carefully.

Or picture the world as a shifting Rubik's Cube. The pieces are always moving, and the colors rarely align. But if you're patient and observant, a moment comes when everything clicks into place—just for a second. That's your opportunity. Most people miss it because they're either rushing ahead or stuck in analysis paralysis. But those who stay present and pay attention can act at just the right time.

Slowing down your reaction time, even briefly, allows you to assess situations more fully. It gives you access to information you wouldn't have otherwise—just like that crucial moment at our event when the right connection appeared because I stayed calm and patient. The more you practice this, the more you start to notice the moments when everything aligns, like synchronicity unfolding.

Some people call this intuition, but it's really just experience meeting awareness—learning to recognize patterns and opportunities that others miss because they're too busy reacting. When you hold your fire, stay calm, and give things a chance to line up, you make better decisions and open the door to smarter solutions.

KNOWING WHEN TO PIVOT

Another aspect of not freaking out is knowing when to pivot. As you continue on your entrepreneurial path, it's natural to feel moments of doubt or uncertainty about whether you're on the right track. Sometimes, staying the course can feel like the only option, but that mindset can keep you from true growth.

One of the hardest lessons in business—and in life—is knowing when to change directions. People often stay stuck because they've already invested time, money, or energy into something, even when it's clearly not working. They think, *I've already put so much into this; I can't quit now.*

In both life and business, we resist change because of sunk costs—the feeling that walking away means losing all the effort we've already put in. But the truth is, staying stuck costs far more in the long run.

I've been there. I stayed in a relationship longer than I probably should have because I felt like I had already invested so much time and energy into it. But deep down, I knew it was working less and less with each passing year. Still, at seventy years old, the thought of starting over felt overwhelming. It was even harder because this person was my closest friend in the world—someone I deeply love, someone who's been with me through thick and thin. But together, we had to face the truth: It wasn't working for either of us. And no matter how much history we shared, that wasn't a good enough reason to stay.

The same applies to business. Maybe you've invested thousands on a marketing strategy that isn't panning out. Or maybe you've spent years building a signature program that no longer excites you—or worse, isn't resonating with your clients. It can be scary, even painful, to shut something down after pouring in so much time, money, and energy—but sometimes letting go is the smartest move you can make.

When I was running IIN, my staff used to get frustrated with how frequently I'd change my mind and shift directions. And I'd think, *Well, yeah, that's because things are always changing.* Business is dynamic. Markets shift, new information comes in, and what worked yesterday might not work tomorrow.

Take Knew Health, for example. We originally started as a marketing company for an existing medical cost-sharing plan. When that company started treating us poorly, we pivoted to another provider. And when that one turned out to be even worse, we pivoted again. That's just how business works: You have to stay present, flexible, and open to change.

GETTING COMFORTABLE WITH MONEY

Just as flexibility and adaptability are key in business strategy, they also apply to your relationship with money. Money has a way of bringing up our deepest fears and insecurities. Some people avoid looking at their finances altogether while others make good money but sabotage their success because, deep down, they don't feel worthy of wealth. The good news is, just like any mindset, you can reshape your relationship with money—and when you do, it can unlock new possibilities for growth, security, and impact.

Getting comfortable with money isn't just about earning more; it's also about navigating the ups and downs that come with it. Business naturally has cycles: busy seasons and slow stretches. It's best not to panic during those slower times. Scarcity mentality can sneak in, leading you to make impulsive decisions out of fear rather than strategy. This is when many entrepreneurs slash prices, overcommit, or say yes to things they should say no to—all because they're afraid the money won't come back.

I've never been purely driven by money or emotionally attached to it. To me, it's just a tool—a man-made currency that comes and goes. My deeper motivation has always been to leave the world better than I found it—to improve people's health and happiness and make a lasting impact. Scientists say money lights up the same brain areas as heroin,[9] but that high is fleeting. Impact, on the other hand, leaves a legacy. That's why I've never let money control me: Doing so would be the greatest sacrifice of all, costing me my freedom. Whether I've been poor or rich, I've always found creative ways to make things work because my purpose goes beyond profit.

It's like that moment in *The Wizard of Oz* when Toto pulls back the curtain and reveals that the big scary wizard is just a man behind a machine. Once you see money for what it really is—a system

9   Ali Venosa, "Financial Planning: How the Brain's Subconscious Can Influence Spending Habits," *Medical Daily*, January 16, 2016, https://www.medicaldaily.com/financial-planning-how-brains-subconcious-can-influence-spending-habits-369822.

created by people—much of the fear and emotion surrounding it fades away.

Learning to stay calm around money—especially when the numbers get big or the income dips—isn't just about managing finances; it's about growing into someone who can handle bigger opportunities and responsibilities. When you stop freaking out about numbers, you start seeing possibilities instead of problems. This shift in mindset is essential as you transition from startup mode to scaling up. Trust the flow, know that slow seasons are temporary, and stay grounded enough to make decisions from a place of confidence, not fear.

DON'T QUIT YOUR DAY JOB

On a related note, when you're starting out as an entrepreneur, it can be tempting to go all in. The idea of quitting your day job and dedicating every moment to your new business sounds thrilling—you want to prove to yourself and the world that you can make it. But for most new entrepreneurs, keeping a steady income while building your business isn't just practical; it's the smartest way to set yourself up for long-term success.

Your day job acts as a safety net, allowing you to take calculated risks rather than desperate ones. Without financial stability, you're more likely to make business decisions from a place of fear instead of strategy because you need to pay the bills. This can lead to burnout, resentment, and ultimately failure.

Many entrepreneurs get excited about the perks of working for themselves—flexible hours, no boss, and the potential for higher earnings—and, in the process, put the cart before the horse. Stories of overnight success can trick you into thinking you're falling behind if you're not all in from the start. But funding your business with your existing income stream is a more sustainable approach.

Consider this: The majority of new businesses fail. Relying on a fledgling business to support you entirely is like stepping outside without an umbrella when there's a 90 percent chance of rain. That's why it makes sense to take things slow. Give yourself time to test and refine your products or services before diving headfirst into the unknown.

Your day job doesn't have to be your dream job. Think of it as a bridge, not your final destination. Whether it's in your current field or something completely unrelated, its role is to support you while you build the thing you care about. Even if it's not fulfilling, it's providing the stability and time you need to grow your business sustainably.

Balancing a day job with building your business might mean cutting back on socializing or working evenings and weekends for a while. But this is temporary. As your business gains traction, you can gradually scale back at your day job—perhaps by transitioning to part-time or reducing your hours. Eventually, you'll be ready to make the leap to full-time entrepreneurship, with the confidence that comes from a solid foundation.

Here are some strategies for balancing both a day job and an entrepreneurial venture:

1. **Time-Blocking:** Schedule dedicated hours for your business outside work, and protect that time fiercely—whether it's early mornings, evenings, or weekends.

2. **Start Small:** Instead of trying to do everything at once, focus on one or two key goals at a time, such as building your website or signing your first client. Small wins build momentum.

3. **Communicate Your Priorities:** Share your plans with your boss, coworkers, friends, and family so they understand your commitments and can support you.

4. **Find Alignment Where You Can:** Leverage skills from your day job to support your entrepreneurial goals. For example, if you work in marketing, use those skills to create a strategic marketing plan for your own business.

Holding on to your day job for now doesn't make you any less of an entrepreneur. If anything, it shows foresight and discipline. By growing your business thoughtfully and with a solid foundation, you're setting it up for long-term success while making sure it aligns with your values and supports your life—not the other way around.

———

When you learn to stay calm in the face of challenges—whether it's a health crisis like I experienced, business setbacks, or any other curveball life throws at you—you create space for growth and innovation. Rather than getting caught up in fear or ego, you can move forward with grounded awareness. You can see opportunities more clearly and make decisions from a place of wisdom rather than reaction. After all, we're all just floating on a rock in space, so there's no point in panicking. Stay open, stay present, and keep your head clear. That's how you'll stay true to your deeper purpose and continue to evolve as both a person and an entrepreneur, which brings us to our final lesson.

REFLECTION QUESTIONS

1. What's one situation in your business that usually triggers an emotional reaction, and how might you respond differently next time?

2. Think of a recent business challenge. What additional perspectives would situational awareness have provided?

3. What upcoming business situation could you prepare for using mental rehearsal?

4. How do emotions about money influence your business decisions?

5. How could maintaining your current job or income source actually support your entrepreneurial dreams rather than hold them back?

10

NEVER STOP GROWING

After mastering the art of staying calm in the face of challenges, the final step in our journey is channeling that composure into meaningful growth. Just like in soccer, where the ball is always moving, business is constantly in motion. If you aren't watching the game closely, you could miss something important. But the best players don't just chase the ball; they anticipate where it's going. They see the whole field: the players, the openings, the bigger game unfolding. Now, it's your turn to step back, see the bigger picture, and grow into the next version of yourself.

In the early stages of building a business, survival is the name of the game. You're focused on getting clients, making sales, and keeping the lights on. But once you find your footing and learn to stay centered under pressure, your perspective expands. You begin to see your business as more than a way to make a living; it becomes a platform for creating change. You start asking bigger questions: *What else is possible? What impact can I make beyond myself?*

That's what this chapter is about: learning how to keep growing without burning out, how to choose the right opportunities, and how to create impact that lasts. It's about playing the long game, making smart, strategic moves, and knowing when to pass and when to take the shot. In the pages ahead, we'll explore how to evolve with intention so your business doesn't just succeed in the short term—it leaves a legacy.

DON'T SWEAT THE SMALL STUFF

To play the long game, you have to know where to focus your energy. Not everything deserves your attention. In business, it's crucial to distinguish between what's truly important and what's just noise. There will always be minor hiccups—an unhappy client, a tech glitch, or a workflow issue. These are just part of running a business. But if you get bogged down by every little problem, you'll miss the bigger threats and opportunities.

While I was CEO at IIN, keeping my eye on the ball meant not obsessing over constantly perfecting the curriculum. The curriculum was solid. We had one hundred top teachers. Whether we added one or two more wasn't going to change the game.

Instead, I had to focus on the big picture: marketing, sales, student satisfaction, and making sure the business continued to grow. If I had spent all my time fine-tuning details that weren't actually driving revenue, IIN would never have scaled the way it did.

The same applies to your business. The real game-changer isn't perfecting the product; it's knowing where to put your time and energy for maximum impact. With experience, you'll learn to tell the difference between what *feels* urgent and what actually matters. When something demands your attention, take a step back and ask:

- Will this still matter in a month?
- Does this directly affect revenue, customer satisfaction, or business growth?
- Is this a one-time inconvenience or a recurring issue?

It's easy to get caught up putting out fires or perfecting details that don't move the needle. But being busy doesn't always mean you're making progress. True success comes from focusing on the actions that actually move your business forward.

INNOVATE OR STAGNATE

Staying focused isn't just about managing what's in front of you; it's about anticipating where the game is headed. Focusing solely on the present can cause you to miss what's coming next. In business, if you're not evolving, you're falling behind. Many businesses start strong but stall when they stop innovating. Just because your business had momentum early on doesn't mean it will keep growing year after year.

When I first launched IIN, holistic health was still emerging, and there were fewer players in the game. But as the industry grew and competition increased, staying relevant meant evolving with the times. Whenever market demand shifted, I didn't cling to what had worked in the past; I looked for new ways to provide value to our students and keep the business thriving.

If I were still running IIN today, I'd be teaching health coaches how to incorporate lab testing, supplements, peptides, exosomes, and stem cell therapy into their practices—areas that reflect where the future of wellness is headed. Business success isn't about sticking to a winning formula forever. It's about adapting to the changing landscape while staying true to what your business is really about.

This doesn't mean chasing every trend. It means staying flexible and open to new ideas while maintaining your core mission. It means paying attention to your audience, continuously learning, and trusting your instincts about what's worth your time and energy. The most successful entrepreneurs aren't just reactive; they're proactive. You need to be ready to pivot when needed—even if the next step isn't completely clear.

EMBRACE SLOW GROWTH

In the rush to scale, it's easy to forget that business success doesn't always need to be a sprint. Many entrepreneurs treat success like a race to some imaginary finish line, pushing themselves to achieve everything as quickly as possible. But business is a long game. Consider this: I'm seventy, and with my high level of self-care combined with parents who lived almost to one hundred, I could have another thirty years ahead of me—the same time span as from twenty to fifty. This is a very long time, yet most people don't realize it. So many entrepreneurs burn themselves out in just a few years, acting as if all their success has to happen immediately. If you take care of yourself and your business, you'll pace yourself for the long run, making your later years more productive and impactful.

What often gets overlooked in the pursuit of rapid success is the toll it can take on your well-being, relationships, and long-term sustainability. Embracing slow growth means choosing a path that aligns with your values and vision, even if it's not the fastest route to the finish line. It means taking the time to build a solid foundation, refining your processes, and ensuring that each step forward is a step that supports the life and business you truly want.

Consider Kara's story. After graduating from IIN, she launched an organic food business from her home that gained a lot of traction in a short period of time. What began as a side hustle in her kitchen suddenly grew into a national phenomenon. Kara was thrilled, but with her rapid success came immense pressure. She found herself juggling increasing product demand, full-time responsibilities, and the challenges of maintaining a business—all while raising young children and managing a marriage. While I could hear the excitement and adrenaline in her voice as she told me all of this, I could also hear her exhaustion.

Kara had fallen into what I call the hero trap—trying to do it all at the expense of her well-being. I reminded her to "follow the speed limit." "Money is replaceable," I said, "but time isn't. Don't do what I did. These precious years with young children won't come back."

Kara had received an offer to sell her business for a life-changing sum of money—an amount that could set her family up for the future. I encouraged her to seriously consider the offer, especially while her product was in high demand, because tomorrow holds no guarantees. She admitted she was thinking about selling but was torn. After much discussion, she realized that holding on to the business might not serve her long-term goals. Ultimately, she chose to prioritize her well-being and family.

Kara's story is a reminder that rapid growth can be exhilarating but also risky. Scaling too quickly without the right systems, team, or support in place can lead to burnout, strained relationships, and a business that feels more like a burden than a blessing. Slow growth, on the other hand, allows you to build a solid foundation. It gives you time to refine your processes, develop your leadership skills, and align your business with your life's priorities.

For highly sensitive entrepreneurs, rapid scaling can feel especially overwhelming. It can disconnect you from why you started your business in the first place. Slow growth, on the other hand, allows you to stay true to your original vision, course correct as needed, and genuinely enjoy the journey. It's not just about pacing yourself; it's about being intentional. It's about asking yourself, *What do I want this business to look like in five or ten years?* and *How can I grow in a way that supports my values and well-being?*

Here are some strategies to help you stay mindful as you grow your business.

PRACTICAL STRATEGIES
FOR CONSCIOUS SCALING

1. **Prioritize Quality over Quantity**: It's better to have one hundred truly happy customers than one thousand who are only a little interested. Focus on giving great value to your main audience rather than trying to reach a larger, less engaged group.

2. **Listen to Your Intuition**: If a growth opportunity feels forced or creates more stress than excitement, it might not be right for you. Pay attention to those inner signals; they're often telling you what you truly need.

3. **Protect Your Time and Energy**: Just like in personal relationships, your business needs clear boundaries. That doesn't only mean turning down misaligned opportunities; it means managing your workload, setting realistic expectations, and making space for what matters to you outside of your career. Protecting your time and energy allows you to stay focused and build a business that supports your well-being.

Remember: True success comes from steady, sustainable progress—not from chasing quick results. Just like raising a child, your business requires care and patience to thrive. Slowing down often leads to more lasting success, allowing you to preserve your energy, maintain quality, protect your personal life, and build a stronger foundation. Business growth is a marathon, not a sprint.

BE SELECTIVE WITH OPPORTUNITIES

Growing sustainably also means being intentional about which opportunities you pursue. As your business grows, more opportunities will come your way, but not all of them will be the right fit. Just because something is possible doesn't mean it aligns with your vision or priorities, so it's important not to jump at every new opportunity that presents itself. Saying yes to everything can dilute your focus, drain your resources, and pull you away from what truly matters. Learning to say no keeps you on track and prevents burnout.

I once worked with an e-commerce company that wasn't content just selling products; they wanted to expand into education by creating online courses. The problem was their core audience consisted of wealthy individuals over fifty-five who were interested in buying products, not signing up for classes. Despite my advice to reconsider, they invested a million dollars into building an online learning platform. As I predicted, it didn't resonate with their audience. At that point, to make it work, they would have needed to spend another million just to attract visitors to the site—without any guarantee that these visitors would convert into paying customers. In the end, this unnecessary project drained time, energy, and money from their profitable core business.

The takeaway? Just because you can pursue an idea doesn't mean you should. Before saying yes to an opportunity, ask yourself, *Does this align with my long-term vision? Does it support my core business? Does it truly serve my customers?*

BEYOND THE PURSUIT OF MORE

Being intentional with your growth means not just evaluating which opportunities to pursue but also evaluating why you pursue growth at all. As you evolve, it's worth examining what truly drives you beyond simply acquiring more.

I've watched so many people get caught up in an endless chase—always pushing for the next big achievement, the next level of recognition, the next milestone of success. It's like we're all running on a treadmill that keeps getting faster, thinking that somehow, the next big thing will finally make us feel complete.

Even after achieving considerable success and wealth, many people keep pushing for more—even when they have more money than they could spend in several lifetimes. It's like they missed the memo that they can't take any of it with them when they die. If I could coach them, I'd ask, "What's really going on here?" Because beneath that relentless drive, there's often fear—fear of not being enough, fear of stillness, fear of losing control. We convince ourselves that success will bring peace, but if we're chasing validation through external achievements, that peace will always be just out of reach.

What I've discovered is that real fulfillment usually comes from doing less, not more. It comes from stripping away the noise and distractions that keep us from seeing what truly matters. At a certain point, I realized that, after having enough to live comfortably, more money wasn't making my life any better. So I started sharing it. In one of my companies, for instance, I've given employees a good share of the company's profits on top of their regular pay. It made a substantial difference in their lives while barely changing anything in mine.

This isn't about being a martyr; it's about shifting from self-centered ambition to purpose-driven living. When we focus on the well-being of others, we break free from the illusion that success is about dominance or accumulation. True leadership is rooted in humility and service, not in proving our worth through relentless achievement. Similarly, true wealth isn't measured by what we acquire but by the positive impact we create, the relationships we nurture, and the peace that comes from aligning with what truly matters.

By embracing this perspective, we move beyond a focus on personal gain and open ourselves to deeper connection, gratitude, and resilience. Life becomes clearer. We make decisions from a place of purpose, not fear. We stop performing and start living—fully, authentically, freely. Success isn't about how much you have; it's about knowing what fulfills you and leaning into that. When you release the pressure to constantly achieve more, you create space for something even more fulfilling: giving back.

THE ART OF GIVING BACK

Giving back has become one of the most meaningful parts of my life. Over the years, I've donated to causes and people I believe in, backing organizations that make real change happen. It's deeply fulfilling to know that my resources can make a real difference. I've been inspired by people like Paul Newman, whose company, Newman's Own, gives 100 percent of its profits to charity. People called Paul generous, but he always said giving was his greatest gift to himself. I couldn't agree more; helping others feels better than any amount of money in the bank.

Your version of giving back doesn't have to look like mine. Maybe for you, it's volunteering at a local community center, mentoring someone, or supporting a friend's small business. It could be as simple as showing up for a neighbor who needs help. The key is finding what aligns with your values and strengths. When you do, giving back isn't just an act of service; it becomes a source of personal fulfillment.

As your business grows, consider how you'll grow beyond yourself. If you had enough money to live comfortably, how might that shift your focus? What do you dream of creating with your one precious life? Whether it's family, impact, legacy, or financial security that enables you to give back, staying connected to your bigger purpose helps you navigate challenges and make decisions with clarity.

Of course, creating lasting impact requires more than good intentions; it demands wisdom in how we manage our resources and relationships. This brings us to another important lesson I've learned along the way.

TRUST, BUT VERIFY

Running a business is like being the captain of a ship: You rely on your crew to handle their duties, but you still need to check the navigation charts and watch the weather. The phrase *trust, but verify* comes from an old Russian proverb, and it's some of the best business advice I've ever received. It reminds us that while trust is essential, so is staying engaged and aware.

This becomes even more important as your business grows. Scaling often requires letting go of certain tasks and trusting others to handle them. That's good—necessary, even. But letting go doesn't mean checking out entirely.

Many business owners swing between extremes. At first, they try to control everything. Then, once they start delegating, they step back too far, assuming someone else is tracking the numbers, managing customer feedback, or keeping operations running smoothly. Months later, they realize their marketing isn't working, customers are unhappy, or finances have slipped off track. The right balance lies somewhere in the middle—trusting your people while staying connected enough to catch issues before they become bigger problems.

VISUALIZATION EXERCISE: YOUR BUSINESS AT SCALE

Close your eyes and imagine your business at five times its current size:

- Who are the key people by your side?
- What areas do you still oversee personally?
- How do you stay connected to your team and customers?
- What systems help you monitor what matters most?

Write down your answers; they'll help guide your growth decisions.

This isn't about micromanaging or doubting your team; it's about being a responsible owner. No one will ever care about your business quite as much as you do, and that's not a bad thing. It's just reality. Staying engaged where it counts ensures nothing slips through the cracks. That means asking questions when things don't add up, keeping an eye on important numbers, regularly checking in with your team and customers, and making sure everyone has what they need to succeed. It means creating simple systems to track what matters and building relationships at all levels of your company. Most importantly, it means staying connected to your company's mission and values. Trust your instincts, trust your people—but keep your eyes open.

EMBRACE THE GRAY AREAS

This balance between trust and verification might seem tricky—even contradictory. But that's the beauty of entrepreneurship. Sometimes, the best path forward isn't black or white; it's somewhere in between.

As your business grows, things usually get more complicated, not less. If there's one thing I hope you take away from this book, it's this: There is no single perfect formula for success. The real difference between those who thrive and those who burn out isn't some magic strategy; it's the ability to stay present, adaptable, and in tune with what's happening, all while keeping your momentum.

At IIN, I included more than one hundred dietary theories in the curriculum—everything from Keto to Paleo to the banana diet—not because any one of them was the ultimate answer, but to show how many different approaches can work. Students would see pretty quickly that for every diet claiming to be the best, there was another one saying the exact opposite. So which one was right?

That was the whole point. There is no one-size-fits-all solution. Real success—whether in health or business—comes from learning to think for yourself, listening to what actually works for you, and staying open to change. I didn't want to hand students a set of rigid rules. I wanted them to develop their own instincts, to trust themselves enough to make smart, informed decisions. Because at the end of the day, no expert, book, or trend knows your body—or your business—better than you do. And just as no single diet works for everyone, no single business strategy guarantees success for every entrepreneur. One person might build a thriving business by doing things one way while someone else succeeds by doing the exact opposite. You've got to find what fits *you*.

You've probably noticed that some things I've said in this book seem to contradict other things. That was intentional—because all of it is true. When you embrace these contradictions and get comfortable in the gray areas, you give yourself room to experiment, adjust, and find what works for you as an individual. The mistake is thinking it has to be either this or that; more often than not, it's both. It's knowing yourself. It's finding a balanced middle path.

YOUR LIFE, YOUR LEGACY

As we reach the end of our journey together, there's one last piece of wisdom I want to share—something my father taught me years ago with a simple bumper sticker on his car. It read, "This is your life, not a dress rehearsal." That wisdom applies to everything: starting your business, growing it, and making sure your success leaves a lasting impact, even when you're no longer in the driver's seat.

Life isn't about waiting until you feel completely ready or have all the answers. You never will—and that's okay. What matters is having the courage to take the first step, knowing you'll face challenges, make mistakes, and keep learning as you go.

Don't be like Stripe, the caterpillar from the start of this book, who climbed and climbed, only to realize he was on the wrong path altogether. Watch out for the trap of "I'll be happy when [fill in the blank]." And try not to measure your success by what someone else has. There will always be someone with more—more money, more followers, more recognition. Chasing that leads nowhere worth going.

Authentic success isn't about outpacing others; it's about aligning your life with what actually matters to you. At the end of the day, we're spiritual beings living in a material world, and the endgame is more than wealth—it's balance, fulfillment, and impact. Make sure the climb you're on is leading somewhere that genuinely feels worth it.

As you spread your wings, try not to lose sight of why you started your business—to create freedom, purpose, and something bigger than a paycheck. Remember, success isn't a destination; it's how you show up each day, authentically, for what matters most. Stay present, stay agile, and trust yourself. Hustle with intention. Hustle with courage. And always—hustle from the heart.

ABOUT THE AUTHOR

JOSHUA ROSENTHAL is an author, wellness visionary, and philanthropist dedicated to transforming how people think about health, healing, and empowerment. Best known as the founder of the Institute for Integrative Nutrition (IIN), he helped bring holistic health and coaching into the mainstream, training hundreds of thousands of wellness professionals worldwide.

His bestselling books—including *Integrative Nutrition: A Whole-Life Approach to Health and Happiness*—have helped shape the global conversation about mind–body wellness. His most recent work, *Heal the Healer*, is a compassionate survival guide for wellness workers and caregivers facing chronic stress, exhaustion, and undervaluation.

Today, Joshua's work extends far beyond education. He helped found Knew Health, a pioneering medical cost-sharing community and health insurance alternative designed for health and wellness-minded individuals. He also advises and invests in mission-driven wellness startups that align with his commitment to healthy living, longevity, collective happiness, and well-being.

A lifelong advocate for spiritual growth and systemic change, Joshua continues to support coaches, healers, and entrepreneurs in building purposeful, profitable ventures that uplift both individuals and communities.